52 Decorative Weekend Woodworking Projects

52 Decorative Weekend Woodworking Projects

John A. Nelson

Sterling Publishing Co., Inc. New York

Dedication

To my wife, Joyce

Acknowledgments

I wish to thank Deborah Porter Hayes for taking all the photographs of the projects; they are just great.

I extend my thanks to John Woodside, Editorial Director, Rodman Neumann, Editor, and the staff at STERLING PUBLISHING CO. who transformed my manuscript and art into this book.

I especially want to thank my wife, Joyce, for typing my scribbling into a readable manuscript, my daughter, Jennifer, for helping paint some of the projects, Bill Bigelow for making seven of the larger projects for me, Greg Morrison who helped my wife set up our computer, and, last but not least, Jim Knight who critiqued each project as I designed and made them.

To the woodworkers who make these projects, I hope you like and enjoy making them.

Library of Congress Cataloging-in-Publication Data

Nelson, John A., 1935–
    52 decorative weekend woodworking projects / John A.
Nelson.
        p.   cm.
    Includes index.
    ISBN 0-8069-0392-9
    1. Woodwork.   I. Title.   II. Title: Fifty-two decorative weekend
woodworking projects.
TT180.N43   1993
684'.08—dc20   93-15288
                                                                          CIP

Edited by R. P. Neumann

10   9   8   7   6   5   4   3   2   1

Published in 1993 by Sterling Publishing Company, Inc.
387 Park Avenue South, New York, N.Y. 10016
© 1993 by John A. Nelson
Distributed in Canada by Sterling Publishing
% Canadian Manda Group, P.O. Box 920, Station U
Toronto, Ontario, Canada M8Z 5P9
Distributed in Great Britain and Europe by Cassell PLC
Villiers House, 41/47 Strand, London WC2N 5JE, England
Distributed in Australia by Capricorn Link Ltd.
P.O. Box 665, Lane Cove, NSW 2066
Manufactured in the United States of America
All rights reserved

Sterling ISBN 0-8069-0392-9

Contents

INTRODUCTION

All the projects in this book are designed to be made over a weekend—all fifty-two of them. A project for each weekend for a full year. I must admit, however, one or two of the projects may require a *long*, three-day weekend. Others can be put together in a weekend, but will need an extra day or two to apply a stain or paint finish. The projects range from very simple to an intermediate woodworking level—something for everyone, I hope!

The projects have been carefully chosen so that most can be made using only basic woodworking tools. A few projects do require a lathe, and one or two require the use of a band or scroll saw. If you do not have those power tools, but would like to make these projects, you might consider enrolling in an evening woodworking class for adults. Most local high schools offer these classes and have the special equipment you will need.

Because each reader will be at a different skill level and each will have completely different tools, only brief and basic instructions for making each project are given in most cases. Most projects are rather simple and, with a little thought and preparation, should be within the skill level of most woodworkers.

Each and every project has been made at least once using the finished plans and drawings so all dimensions *should* be correct by now. We have checked and rechecked each dimension and all the detail illustrations, but Murphy's law will surely prevail, so *please* recheck each dimension again before you make any cuts yourself.

Using the Drawings for Each Project

With each project there is at least a two-view drawing provided. One is almost always called the *front view,* and the other is either the *side view* or the *top view.* These views are positioned in a standard way; the front view is always the most important view and the place you should start in studying the drawings. The side view is located directly to the *right* of the front view; the top view is located directly *above* the front view.

At times a *section view* is used to further illustrate some particular feature(s) of the project. The section view is sometimes a partial view that illustrates only a portion of the project such as a particular moulding detail or way of joining parts.

Most of the projects also have an *exploded view,* which fully illustrates how the project goes together. Make sure that *you* fully understand how the project is to be assembled *before* any work is started.

The drawings throughout this book *number* each and every part. Each part is called-off in as many views as possible so that you can see *exactly* where each part is located. A box accompanies each set of drawings that serves as a *bill of materials* list. Each part is listed, *in order,* using the same number *and* noting its name, its overall size, and exactly *how many* of each part is required.

Multiple parts should be made exactly the same size and shape. Every now and then a project requires a *pair* of parts, that is, a right-hand piece and a left-hand piece. In such a case, take care not to make duplicate pieces, but rather a left-hand and right-hand pair. In most projects requiring a pair, this is noted—but for any "multiple" parts double-check if in doubt.

Throughout, when practical, I numbered all the parts in the order that I would *suggest* you make and assemble them. You might want to make and assemble your project some other way, but this is what worked best for me and is how I made it.

Making the Project

After you thoroughly study the project, start by carefully making each individual part. Take care to make each piece exactly to the correct size and exactly *square*—that is, each cut at 90 degrees to the face—as required.

Sand each individual piece, but take care to keep all the edges sharp— **do not round the edges** at this time—some will be rounded *after* assembly.

After all the pieces have been made with great care, "dry-fit" the pieces— that is, cautiously put together the entire project to check for correct fit throughout before final assembly. If anything needs refitting, this is the time to correct it.

When the pieces all fit correctly, glue and/or nail the project together, again taking care that all fits are tight and square. Sand the project all over; it is at this time that edges can be "rounded," if necessary. The project is then ready for finishing.

Today, the trend is towards using the metric system of measure; therefore, a Metric Conversion chart is provided for quick conversion on page 158.

Enlarging a Pattern or Design

Many of the drawings are reduced relative to the actual size of the parts so that all of the information can be presented on the page. In some projects, the patterns for irregular parts or irregular portions of parts must be enlarged to full size. A grid of squares is drawn over these parts and the original size of the grid is noted on the drawing.

There are four ways a design or shape of the irregular part or parts can be enlarged to full size.

Method One

One of the simplest and most inexpensive ways is to use an ordinary office-type photocopy machine. Most of these newer machines have an enlarging/ reducing feature. Simply put the book page on the machine, choose the enlargement mode you need (usually expressed as a percentage of the original), and make a copy. In extreme cases, you may have to make *another* copy of the enlargement copy in order to get the required size—sometimes you must make more than two copies. In some cases you will not be able to get the exact required size but the result will be close enough for most work, perhaps requiring a little touching up, at most.

Method Two

A very quick and extremely accurate method is to go to a local commercial "Quick-Printer" and ask them to make a P.M.T. (photomechanical transfer) of the area needed to be enlarged or reduced. This is a photographic method that yields an *exact* size without any difficulty. This method will cost about five to fifteen dollars, depending on the size of the final P.M.T.—if your time is valuable, it might be worth the cost.

Method Three

Another simple, quick method is to use a drawing tool called the *pantograph*. It is an inexpensive tool that is very simple to use for enlarging or reducing to almost any required size. If you do a lot of enlarging or reducing, the cost of this tool may be well worth the price.

Method Four

Most authors assume woodworkers will use the grid and dot-to-dot method. It is very simple; you do not have to be an artist to use the method. This method can be used to enlarge or reduce to *any size* or scale. This method requires eight simple steps:

♦ **Step 1:** Note what size the full-size grid should be—this is usually indicated on the drawing near the grid. Most of the grids used with the project drawings must be redrawn so that each square is one-half inch or one inch per side.

♦ **Step 2:** Calculate the overall required width and height. If it is *not* given, simply count the squares across and down and multiply by the size of each square. For example, a one-half-inch grid with 15 squares across requires an overall width of 7½ inches. The paper size needed to draw the pattern full size should be a little larger than the overall size of the part.

♦ **Step 3:** Note: It would be helpful if you have a few basic drafting tools, but not necessary. Tools suggested are: a drafting board, a scale (ruler), a T-square, a 45-degree triangle, masking tape, and a sheet of paper a little larger than the required overall size of the pattern. Tape the paper to the drafting board or other surface and carefully draw the required grid on the paper using the drafting tools or whatever tools you have.

♦ **Step 4:** On the original reduced drawing in the book, start from the upper left corner and add *letters* across the top of the grid from left to right, A through whatever letter it takes to get to the other side of the grid. From the same starting point, add *numbers* down, from 1 to whatever number it takes to get to the bottom of the grid.

♦ **Step 5:** On your full-size grid, add letters and numbers in exactly the same way as the original.

♦ **Step 6:** On the original reduced drawing, draw dots along the pattern outline wherever it crosses the grid.

◆**Step 7:** On your full-size grid, locate and draw the same dots on the grid. It is helpful to locate each dot by using the letters across the top and the numbers along the side. For example, a dot at B-6 can easily be found on the new, full-size grid by coming down from line B and over on line 6.

◆**Step 8:** All that is left to do is to connect the dots. Note: you do not have to be exact, all you have to do is to sketch a line between the dots using your eye to approximate the shape of the original reduced drawing.

Transferring the Pattern from Paper to Wood

Tape the full-size pattern to the wood with carbon paper in between for transferring the pattern. If you are going to copy the pattern many times, make a template instead. Simply transfer the pattern onto a sheet of heavy cardboard or ⅛-inch-thick hardboard or plywood and cut out the pattern. This template can then be used over and over by simply tracing around the template to lay out the pattern for each copy.

If the pattern is symmetrical—that is, the exact same size and shape on both sides of an imaginary line—make only a *half-pattern* and trace it twice, once on each side of the midline. This will ensure the perfect symmetry of the finished part.

For small patterns—8½ inches by 11 inches or smaller at full size—make a photocopy of the full-size pattern using any copy machine. Tape the copy, printed side down, and using a hot flatiron or hot wood-burning set, heat the back side of the copy. The pattern will transfer from the paper directly to the wood. This method is very good for very small or complicated patterns.

Again, for small patterns—8½ inches by 11 inches or smaller at full size—make a photocopy of the pattern. Using rubber cement or spray-mount adhesive, lightly glue the copy directly to the wood. Cut out the piece with the copy glued directly to the wood. Simply peel the copy from the wood *after* you cut out the piece. Then sand all over.

Selecting Material for Your Project

As lumber will probably be the most expensive material you will purchase for each project, it is a good idea that you have some basic knowledge about lumber so that you can make wise choices and save a little money here and there on your purchases.

All lumber is divided into two kinds, hardwood and softwood. Hardwoods are deciduous trees, trees that flower and lose their leaves seasonally; softwoods are the coniferous trees, which are cone-bearing and mostly evergreen. In actuality, a few "hardwoods" are softer than some "softwoods"—but on the whole, hardwoods are harder, closer grained, much more durable, tougher to work, and take a stain beautifully. Hardwood typically costs more than softwood, but it is well worth it.

All wood contains pores—open spaces that served as water-conducting vessels—which are more noticeable in some kinds than in others. Woods such as oak and mahogany have pores that are very noticeable and probably should be filled, for the best finished appearance. Woods such as maple and birch have what is called close-grain, which provides a beautiful smooth finish.

The *grain* of wood is the result of each year's growth of new cells. Around the tree's circumference each year annular growth forms a new and hard fibrous layer. Growth in most trees is seasonal but somewhat regular, so that these rings are evenly spaced. In other trees this annular growth is not very regular, thus creating uneven spacing and thickness. The patterns formed by the rings when the tree is cut into lumber is what we see as the grain pattern.

The softwoods I used for most of the projects are pine, spruce, and fir. Pine was the favorite since it is the easiest to work, especially for simple accessories such as those found in this book. The hardwoods I used most were maple, walnut, oak, cherry, poplar, and birch.

Always buy "dried" lumber, as "green" lumber will shrink, twist, and warp while drying. Purchase the best lumber you can find for these projects since each of them does not take much material at all. Your work will be much easier and the finished project will be so much better for the better quality wood. The actual cost difference between an inexpensive piece of wood and the best you can find will be quite small since the overall cost of any of these projects is very low to begin with.

A few projects call for wide boards. I believe the project would look best if you could find the correct width. The correct width also adds to the authenticity. If this is not possible, glue narrower boards together by edge-joining them to produce the necessary width. Try to match grain patterns with great care so that each joint will not be so noticeable. Even though I prefer the look of the single wide board, I should point out that a glued joint is as strong as a single piece of wood and probably will not warp.

Kinds of Joint

The projects require four kinds of joint—and, for the most part, only three. These basic joints are the *butt joint,* the *rabbet joint,* the *dado joint* and, in a few instances, the *dovetail joint*. These can be made by hand, without power tools. If you do have the power tools, use them; early crafters would have used them if *they* had them.

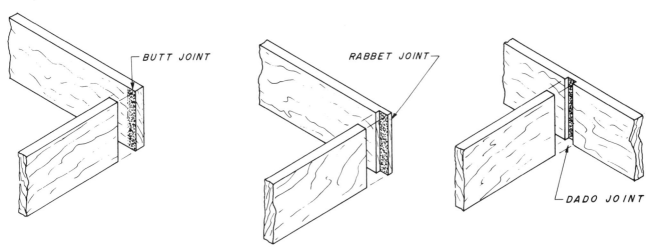

BUTT JOINT

RABBET JOINT

DADO JOINT

Most of the simpler projects use the *butt joint.* This is the simplest of all joints and, as its name implies, is simply two boards that are butted up against each other and joined together, perhaps with glue and nails or screws. The major disadvantage of the butt joint is that there is less surface area available for gluing or nailing than for other joints. Nails sometimes back out of the joint over time, which also makes an opening at the joint. A *rabbet joint* is an L-shaped cutout made along the edge or end of one board to overlap the edge or end of the mating board. This joint can also be nailed and/or glued together. Because rabbet joints are often cut into side pieces, the nails—put in from the sides—may be hidden somewhat from view. *Dado joints* are similar to rabbet joints, except that the cut is made leaving wood shoulders on both sides. A drawer side is an excellent example of the use of both a dado joint and a rabbet joint.

COMBINATION USE OF JOINTS

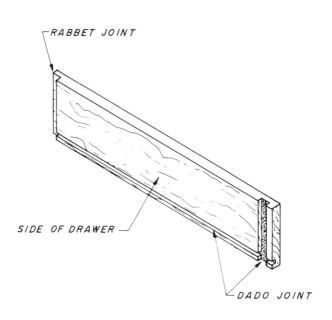

RABBET JOINT

SIDE OF DRAWER

DADO JOINT

Gluing

Glue was not in general use until after 1750. Therefore, most of the projects featured in this book probably were simply nailed together. If by chance they were glued together, they were probably glued together with "hot" animal—or hide—glue.

Wood glues are either "hot" or "cold" glue, depending whether or not heat is used to prepare them. The "hot" glue is made from animal parts, which make the glue very strong and quick-setting. Until very recently old-fashioned hide glue was considered the *only* true, satisfactory kind of glue to use in cabinetmaking. Recent developments in new and better "cold" glues have made this generalization debatable. Cold glues are all derived from synthetic material of one kind or another. They vary in durability and strength. For the simpler projects cold glue is, by far, the easiest to use, and I recommend its use. In using cold glue, always follow the instructions given on the label.

When gluing, always take care to clean all excess glue from around the joint. This is a *must* if you are going to stain the project. The excess glue will not take the stain and will appear white. I find that by waiting for 10 to 15 minutes, just until the glue is almost set, I can carefully remove most of it with a sharp wood chisel. Do not wipe off the excessive glue with a wet cloth as the water will weaken the glue joint and possibly spread glue into the pore space irretrievably, staining the wood.

For the few projects that are a little difficult to hold together properly while gluing, the new hot-glue guns can be very helpful. Hot-glue guns use solid glue sticks that are inserted, heated to their melting point, and then liquid glue is pushed through the tip while very hot. This kind of glue dries very quickly and sets in about 10 seconds without clamping. Take care if you use this kind of glue as it is difficult to get good tight-fitting joints every time. The glue sets up so quickly that you have to work very quickly. This kind of glue is good to use for special applications but not for everything; the slower-drying cold glue is still better to use for most of the projects.

Finishing

Once you have completed assembling your project, you are then ready to apply a finish. This is the important part and should not be rushed. Remember, this is the part that will make the biggest impression for many years to come. No matter how good the wood and hardware you use, regardless of how good the joints are, a poor finish will ruin your project. If it takes eight hours to make the project, plan on eight hours to finish it correctly.

Preparing

◆ **Step 1:** All joints should be checked for tight fits. If necessary apply water putty to all joints—allow ample time for drying. As these are "country" projects, it is not necessary to set and fill the nail heads as most of the originals were left with the nail heads showing. If, however, you do not want to see the nail heads, then set and apply water putty to fill those nail heads, also.

◆ **Step 2:** Sand the project all over in the direction of the wood grain. If sanding is done by hand, use a sanding block, and be careful to keep all corners still *sharp*. Sand all over using an 80 grit sandpaper. Resand all over using a 120 grit sandpaper, and, if necessary, sand once more with 180 grit sandpaper. Take care not to "round" edges at this time.

◆ **Step 3:** If you do want any of the edges rounded, use the 120 grit sandpaper, and later the 180 grit sandpaper, specifically to round the edges.

◆ **Step 4:** I personally think the "country" projects should look old. A copy of an antique that looks new seems somehow to be a direct contradiction. Distressing—making the piece look old—can be done in many ways. Using a piece of coral stone about three inches in diameter, or a similar object, roll the stone across the various surfaces. Don't be afraid to add a few random scratches here and there, especially on the bottom or back, where an object would have been worn the most. Carefully study the object, and try to imagine how it would have been used through the years. Using a rasp, judiciously round the edges where you think wear would have occurred. Resand the entire project and the new "worn" edges with 180 grit paper.

♦ **Step 5:** Clean all surfaces with a damp rag to remove all dust.

Fillers

A paste filler should be used for porous wood such as oak, ash, or mahogany. Purchase paste filler that is slightly darker than the color of your wood as the new wood you used will turn darker with age. Before using paste filler, thin it with turpentine so it can be applied with a brush. Use a stiff brush, and brush with the grain in order to fill the pores. Wipe off with a piece of burlap across the grain after 15 or 20 minutes, taking care to leave filler in the pores. Apply a second coat if necessary; let it dry for 24 hours.

Staining

There are two major kinds of stain: water-base stain and oil-base stain. Water stains are commonly purchased in powder form and mixed as needed by dissolving the powder in hot water. Premixed water-base stains have recently become available. Water stain has a tendency to raise the grain of the wood, so that after it dries, the surface should be lightly sanded with fine sandpaper. Oil stain is made from pigments ground in linseed oil and does not raise the grain.

♦ **Step 1:** Test the stain color on a scrap piece of the same kind of lumber to make certain it will be the color you wish.

♦ **Step 2:** Wipe or brush on the stain as quickly and as even as possible to avoid overlapping streaks. If a darker finish is desired, apply more than one coat of stain. Try not to apply too much stain on the end grain. Allow to dry in a dust-free area for at least 24 hours.

Finishes

Shellac is a hard, easy-to-apply finish and dries in a few hours. For best results, thin slightly with alcohol and apply an extra coat or two. Several coats of thin shellac are much better than one or two thick coats. Sand lightly with extra-fine sandpaper between coats, but be sure to rub the entire surface with a dampened cloth. Strive for a smooth, satin finish—not a high-gloss finish coat—for that "antique" effect.

Varnish is easy to brush on and dries to a smooth, hard finish within 24 hours. It makes an excellent finish that is transparent and will give a deep finish look to your project. Be sure to apply varnish in a completely dust-free area. Apply one or two coats directly from the can with long, even strokes. Rub between each coat, and after the last coat, with 0000 steel wool.

Oil finishes are especially easy to use for projects such as those in this book. Oil finish is easy to apply, long-lasting, never needs resanding, actually improves wood permanently. Apply a heavy, wet coat uniformly to all surfaces, and let set for 20 or 30 minutes. Wipe completely dry until you have a pleasing finish.

Painted Projects

Use a high-quality paint, either oil or water base. Today, the trend is towards water-base paint. Prime your project, and lightly sand after it dries. Apply two *light* coats of paint rather than one thick coat. I like to add some water to thin water-base paint since I feel that water-base paint tends to be a little thick. For all projects for children, be sure to use a nontoxic paint at all times.

Note: For a very satisfying "feel" to the finish and professional touch to your project, apply a top-coat of paste wax as the final step.

Achieving a 150-Year-Old Look

Follow the five steps outlined for preparing your project as described above under finishing. Then follow these steps to distress your project.

♦ **Step 1:** Seal the wood with a light coat of shellac with 50% alcohol. After the shellac is dry, rub lightly with 0000 steel wool. Wipe clean.

♦ **Step 2:** Apply an even coat of oil-base paint, taking care to use an antique color paint. Let dry for 48 hours. Do not paint the backs or bottoms—these were seldom painted on the original pieces.

♦ **Step 3:** Sand with 120 grit sandpaper all the rounded edges you prepared for "wear" marks in "Preparing" step 4. Remember, if these edges were worn, the paint surely would have been removed, also. Sand away paint from all sharp edges and corners since edges and corners would wear through the years.

♦ **Step 4:** Lightly sand all over to remove any paint gloss, using 180 grit sandpaper. Wipe clean.

♦ **Step 5:** Wipe on a *wash coat* of oil-base, black paint with a cloth directly from the can. Take care to get the black paint in all corners, and in all distress marks and scratches. Don't forget the unpainted back and bottoms. Wipe all paint off immediately before it dries, but leave black paint in all corners, joints, scratches, and distress marks. If you apply too much, wipe off using a cloth with turpentine on it. Let dry for 24 hours. Apply a light coat of paste wax.

Alternative One

For that "extra" aged look, apply two coats of paint—each a totally different color; for example, first coat, a powder blue; second coat, antique brick red. Allow 24 hours between coats. After the second coat has dried for 48 hours or more, follow steps 3 and 4 above, but sand the top coat off so that the first color shows through here and there, in layers at worn areas. Finish up with step 5 as outlined above. This is especially good on projects such as footstools or large painted wall boxes.

Alternative Two

If you want your painted project to have a "crackled" finish, follow these additional steps. After step 1 above, apply a coat of liquid hide glue over the intended painted surfaces. Let dry four to twelve hours. Then paint on a coat of gesso (a form of base paint in use since the sixteenth century). Paint lightly and do not go over any strokes. In 10 to 15 seconds, the gesso will start to crackle. Let dry for 24 hours in a very dry area. After 24 hours or more, continue on to step 2 above. (It would be a good idea to experiment on scrap wood before applying any of this to your finished project. Some craftworkers combine step 2 with the crackling by mixing their paint with the gesso, two parts gesso to one part paint.)

Visits to museums, antique shops, and flea markets will help you develop an eye for exactly what an original antique looks like. This will give you an excellent idea of how antiques were worn through the years. With this firsthand experience, you will have a much clearer idea of what kind of finish you are after, so that your careful reproduction will realistically look 150 years old.

THE 52 DECORATIVE PROJECTS

TOYS/GAMES

1 ♦ Elephant Pull Toy

Here is a copy of an antique pull toy. It brought happiness to children years ago as it will bring happiness to children today.

Instructions

♦ **Step 1**   Draw a full-size ½-inch grid on a sheet of heavy paper that is about 6 inches by 9 inches. Lay out the body, part number 1, on the grid.

♦ **Step 2**   Transfer the full-size pattern of the body, part number 1, to the wood, and cut out the body.

♦ **Step 3**   Cut out the ears, parts number 2, and glue them to the body.

♦ **Step 4**   Cut the base, part number 3, and drill holes for the two screws, parts number 6. Locate and drill a hole for the pull string, part number 7.

♦ **Step 5**   Carefully drill two ³⁄₁₆-inch-diameter holes through the sides for the axles (1¾ inches in from the ends).

♦ **Step 6**   Cut the wheels, parts number 4, from a 1½-inch-diameter dowel, ½-inch thick. Drill a ³⁄₁₆-inch-diameter hole in the middle of each wheel.

♦ **Step 7**   Cut the axles, parts number 5, to length.

♦ **Step 8**   Glue and screw the body, part number 1, to the base, part number 3.

♦ **Step 9**   Add the axles, parts number 5, and glue the wheels, parts number 4, to the axles. Take care *not* to glue the wheels to the base.

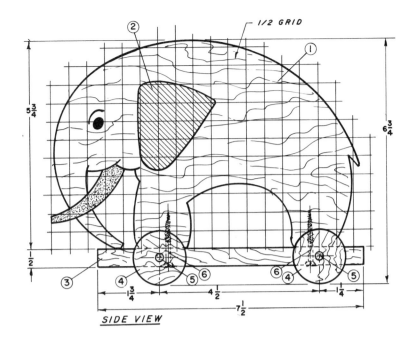

1/2 GRID

SIDE VIEW

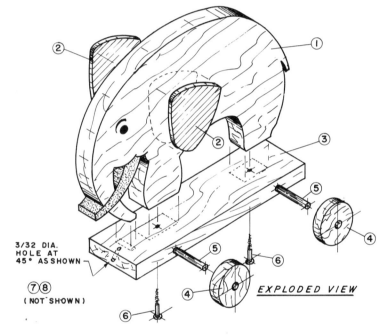

3/32 DIA.
HOLE AT
45° AS SHOWN

7 8
(NOT SHOWN)

EXPLODED VIEW

NO.	NAME	SIZE	REQ'D.
1	BODY	3/4 X 5 3/4-8 5/8	1
2	EAR	1/8 X 2 1/4 - 2 1/2 LG.	2
3	BASE	1/2 X 2 - 7 1/2 LG.	1
4	WHEEL	1 1/2 DIA. - 1/2 THICK	4
5	AXLE	3/16 DIA. - 3 1/4 LG.	2
6	SCREW - FL. HD.	NO. 6 — 1 1/2 LONG	2
7	STRING	LENGTH TO SUIT	1
8	PULL	1/2 DIA. - 3 LONG	1

♦Step 10   Use your imagination and paint your elephant as you see it. Be sure to use nontoxic paint. You can paint the elephant very plain, as was the original, with a lot of detail. Paint the base and wheels with bright colors. Add the pull string, part number 7, and pull, part number 8. Your toy is ready for years of fun.

2 ◆ Dovetail Puzzle

Last year I saw a photograph in a book of a block like this that was made by someone around 1875. I studied the photograph but couldn't figure how it was done. So I made a photocopy of the photograph of the block. The next day I assigned the "problem" to the advanced vocational drafting and design class that I was then teaching. After three or four hours, I came up with the solution myself. In a few days three out of the sixteen students arrived at the same solution that I had. So we *think* this is the way the original was constructed. Even if we are wrong, it makes a *great* conversation piece.

Instructions

The puzzle is made of two *identical* pieces. It is best to make it out of two different kinds of hardwood. Walnut and maple would be an excellent choice.

◆ **Step 1**   Cut two blocks of wood to *exactly* 2 inches by 2 inches and 4¾ inches long.

◆ **Step 2**   Notch a dovetail as illustrated.

◆ **Step 3**   Thin the dovetail to ⅛ inch thick as illustrated.

◆ **Step 4**   Using the dovetail from one block, transfer the *exact* shape to the other block. Using a sharp chisel, notch out the dovetail ⅛ inch deep, as shown.

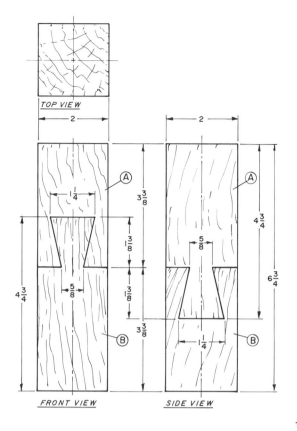

TOP VIEW

2

2

Ⓐ

Ⓐ

$3\frac{3}{8}$

$4\frac{3}{4}$

$1\frac{1}{4}$

$\frac{3}{8}$

$\frac{5}{8}$

$\frac{3}{8}$

$6\frac{3}{4}$

$4\frac{3}{4}$

$\frac{3}{8}$

$\frac{5}{8}$

$1\frac{1}{4}$

Ⓑ

Ⓑ

MATERIAL:
(2) 2 X 2 - 4 3/4 LG.

FRONT VIEW

SIDE VIEW

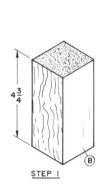

$4\frac{3}{4}$

Ⓑ

STEP 1

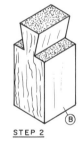

Ⓑ

STEP 2

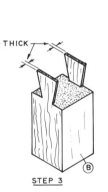

$\frac{1}{8}$ THICK

Ⓑ

STEP 3

TAPER SLIGHTLY

$\frac{1}{8}$ DEEP

Ⓑ

STEP 4

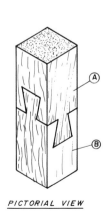

Ⓐ

"ROUND" TIP TO 1/32 THICK

Ⓑ

STEP 5

♦ **Step 5**   Round the top-*inside* edge of the dovetails, as shown.

♦ **Step 6**   Add glue to both parts, and, using a wood vise, *slowly* press the two pieces together. The dovetails will bend out and will snap into place at the last moment. Clamp the dovetails tightly in place until the glue sets.

♦ **Step 7**   Sand all over.

♦ **Step 8**   Apply a high-gloss finish, and when dry, lightly sand with 400-grit sandpaper. Apply a coat of paste wax.

Now show this to woodworking friends and ask them to make one just like it.

Ⓐ

Ⓑ

PICTORIAL VIEW

3 ♦ Nail Puzzle

Here is a great puzzle. At first everyone will say it is absolutely impossible to do! The problem is to balance all 10 nails on top of the middle nail. The balanced nails cannot touch anything and must all be balanced above the head of the center nail. Simple—any *genius* can do it!

Instructions

♦ **Step 1**   Cut the three wood blocks, parts number 1 and 2, to size and sand all over.

♦ **Step 2**   Carefully glue the three wood blocks together as shown.

♦ **Step 3**   Using a router and a ³⁄₁₆-inch radius cove cutter with a ball-bearing follower, make a cut along the top edge.

♦ **Step 4**   Carefully *locate* the eleven holes using the given dimensions in the top view.

♦ **Step 5**   Drill the ten *outer* holes so that an 8 penny common nail will fit *loosely*. Drill the center hole so that an 8 penny common nail will fit tightly.

♦ **Step 6**   Finish all over with a high-gloss finish. Sand all over and add a coat of paste wax.

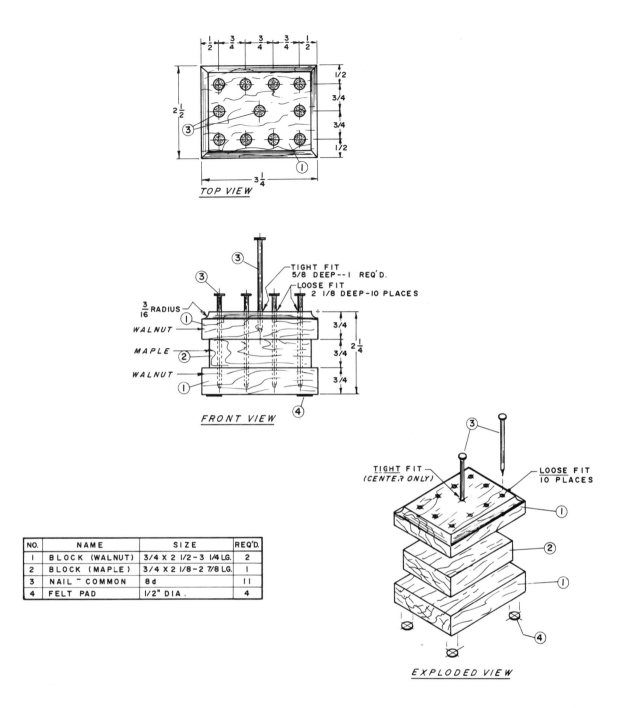

TOP VIEW

FRONT VIEW

EXPLODED VIEW

NO.	NAME	SIZE	REQ'D.
1	BLOCK (WALNUT)	3/4 X 2 1/2 - 3 1/4 LG.	2
2	BLOCK (MAPLE)	3/4 X 2 1/8 - 2 7/8 LG.	1
3	NAIL - COMMON	8 d	11
4	FELT PAD	1/2" DIA.	4

◆**Step 7**   Add the center nail, part number 3, making it a tight fit. Add the 4 felt pads, parts number 4. Clean out the ten outer holes so the 10 nails can be inserted and removed easily. You're ready to test your puzzle.

Before looking at the answer, try to balance the 10 nails on the head of the center nail.

Solution: See the four steps on page 157 for the answer. Have fun!

4 ♦ Toy Snake

Here is a toy that children seem to like. You can be as imaginative as you wish in finishing your snake. Be sure to use nontoxic paint.

Instructions

♦ **Step 1**   Lay out full size the head, part number 2, and tail, part number 3. Transfer them to the wood and cut out.

♦ **Step 2**   Cut six or so body pieces, parts number 1, to overall size.

♦ **Step 3**   Cut the notch and tine according to the given dimensions. It is a good idea to use some kind of a jig so that all notches and tines will be exactly the same size as when standard finger joints are cut.

♦ **Step 4**   Locate and drill the ⅛-inch-diameter holes using the given dimensions.

♦ **Step 5**   Round the ends as shown. Round the inner surfaces with a rasp. Remember, this is a Folk Art, handmade toy, it does *not* have to be exact. "Exact" you can get made out of plastic in a toy store. Sand all pieces.

♦ **Step 6**   Give your pieces a thin base coat of paint. It is easier to paint the pieces now rather than after they are put together.

♦ **Step 7**   Cut the pins, parts number 4, to size.

♦ **Step 8**   Glue the pins to the two *outer* finger joints of the body, part number 1, and tail, part number 3. Take care *not* to get glue on the center finger joint. Check that each joint moves freely.

♦ **Step 9**   Sand all over. Round the edges along the body tail and head, slightly.

♦ **Step 10**   Here is the *fun* part. Paint your snake to make it look as real as possible. Wait till the children see *this* project.

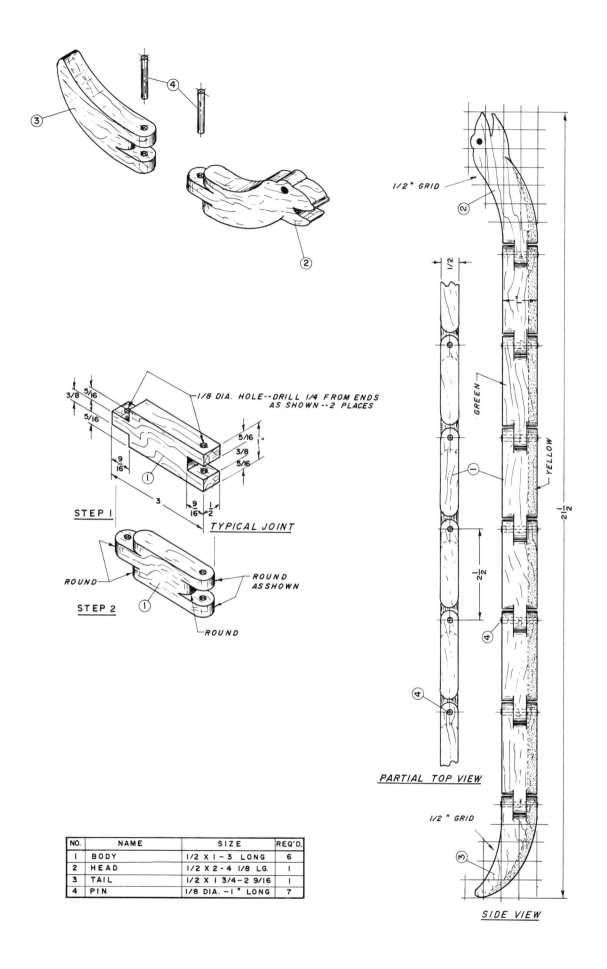

① ④

③

② ④

1/2" GRID

② GREEN

YELLOW

1/2

5/16
3/8
5/16
1/8 DIA. HOLE--DRILL 1/4 FROM ENDS
AS SHOWN--2 PLACES

5/16"
3/8
5/16

9/16
①

3
9/16 1/2

STEP 1

TYPICAL JOINT

ROUND
ROUND
AS SHOWN
①
STEP 2
ROUND

①

2 1/2

④

④

④

21 1/2

PARTIAL TOP VIEW

1/2" GRID

③

SIDE VIEW

NO.	NAME	SIZE	REQ'D.
1	BODY	1/2 X 1 - 3 LONG	6
2	HEAD	1/2 X 2 - 4 1/8 LG.	1
3	TAIL	1/2 X 1 3/4 - 2 9/16	1
4	PIN	1/8 DIA. - 1" LONG	7

5♦Dog Seat

Here is a neat project for any child's room. Most children like dogs, so here is one that will earn its keep. Its width can be changed slightly to accommodate the size of the child you want to make it for. The finished project pictured has an 8-inch seat. This would be for a very small toddler.

Instructions

♦**Step 1**   Lay out the side, part number 1, using a 1-inch grid, and cut out two sides. Locate and drill the six holes for the screws, parts number 4 and 5. Sand all over.

♦**Step 2**   Cut the back, part number 2, two supports, parts number 3, and seat, part number 4, to size. Sand all over.

♦**Step 3**   Glue and screw the two supports, parts number 3, to the sides, parts number 1.

♦**Step 4**   Glue and screw the back, part number 2, and seat, part number 4, in place. Take care to keep everything square. Be sure all four feet sit flat on the bench.

♦**Step 5**   Paint to suit, using nontoxic paint. Your project is now ready to put to use.

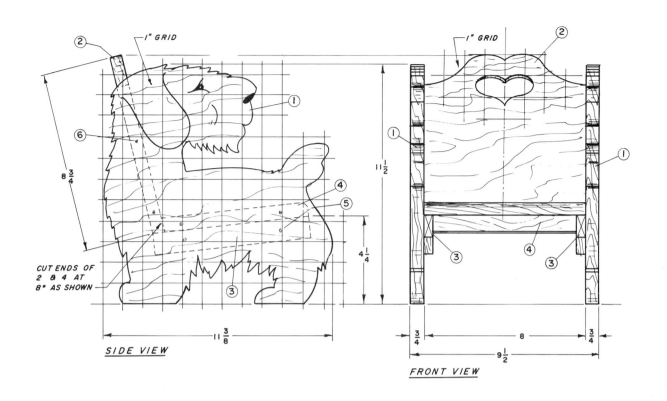

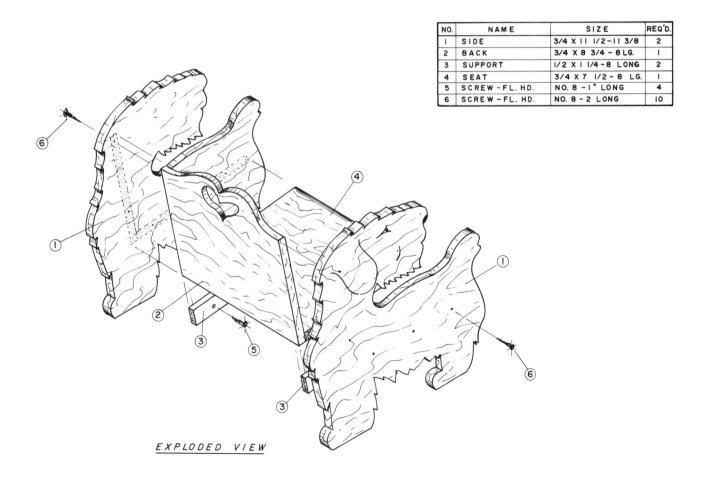

SIDE VIEW

FRONT VIEW

EXPLODED VIEW

NO.	NAME	SIZE	REQ'D.
1	SIDE	3/4 X 11 1/2 - 11 3/8	2
2	BACK	3/4 X 8 3/4 - 8 LG.	1
3	SUPPORT	1/2 X 1 1/4 - 8 LONG	2
4	SEAT	3/4 X 7 1/2 - 8 LG.	1
5	SCREW - FL. HD.	NO. 8 - 1" LONG	4
6	SCREW - FL. HD.	NO. 8 - 2 LONG	10

27

6 ◆ Checkers Game

Believe it or not, the game of Chinese checkers was *not* invented in China; it was invented many years ago by a Swede. Today it still is a popular game.

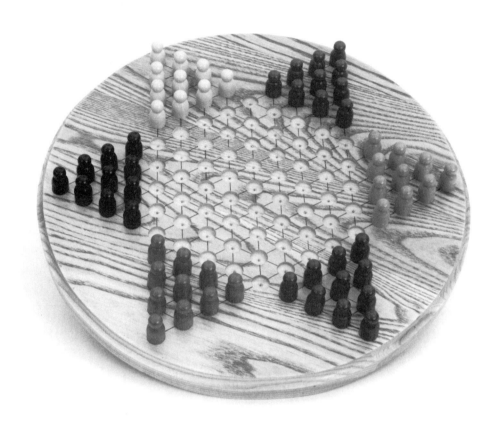

Instructions

◆ **Step 1**   On heavy paper, lay out the grid for the hole locations. The sheet should be about 16 inches square or so. It would be helpful if you have a drafting board, T-square, and 30-degree/60-degree triangle.

◆ **Step 2**   Refer to the drawings for each step to locate the holes. Draw horizontal and vertical lines through the middle of the paper. At the center, draw a circle using a 6^{15}/$_{16}$-inch radius. Divide the circle into three equal parts. Make a triangle with 12-inch sides. Make another triangle (upside down) with 12-inch sides. Divide each leg of both triangles into 1-inch spaces. Draw parallel lines from point to point as shown. Where the points cross is the exact center point for each hole.

◆ **Step 3**   Tape or glue your pattern to a piece of wood that is approximately 16 inches square. Be sure it cannot move. Using a prick punch, ice pick or similar tool, prick punch each of the 121 hole centers.

◆ **Step 4**   Remove the pattern and locate the center hole. From this point, swing a 7¾-inch radius for the outside edge. Cut and sand the outer edge.

28

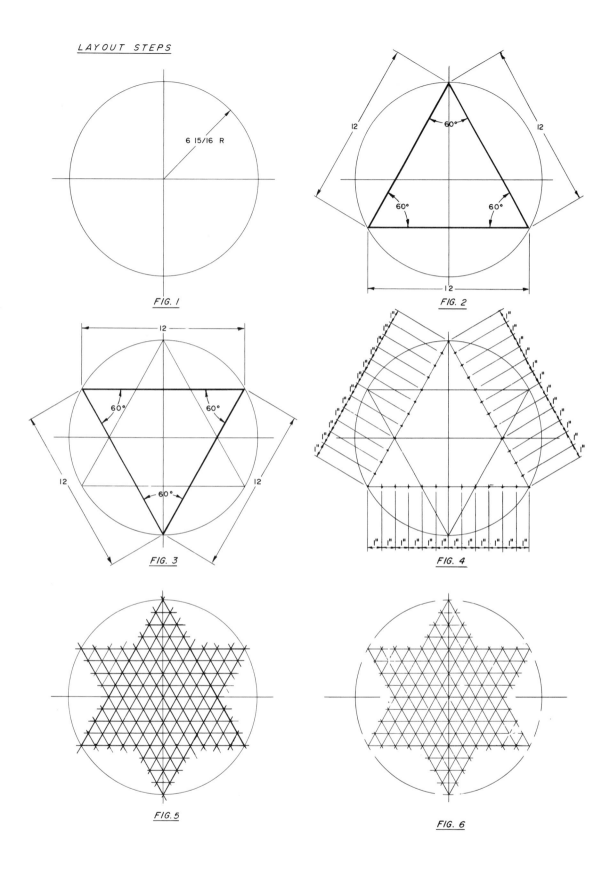

FIG. 1

FIG. 2

FIG. 3

FIG. 4

FIG.5

FIG. 6

♦**Step 5**   Using a ¼-inch radius cove cutter with a ball-bearing follower, make the cove cut around the upper, outer edge, as shown.

♦**Step 6**   Sand all over. (Continued on next page.)

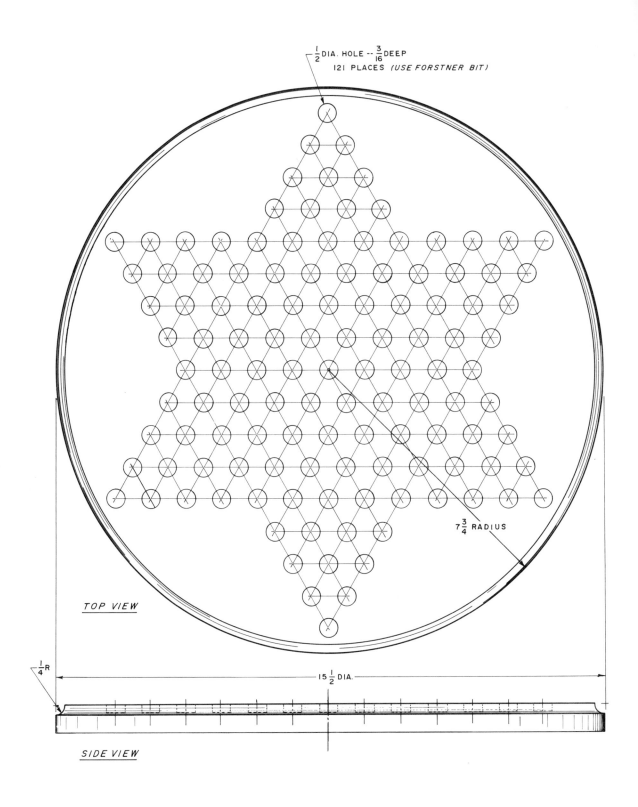

$\frac{1}{2}$ DIA. HOLE -- $\frac{3}{16}$ DEEP
121 PLACES *(USE FORSTNER BIT)*

$7\frac{3}{4}$ RADIUS

TOP VIEW

$\frac{1}{4}$ R

15 $\frac{1}{2}$ DIA.

SIDE VIEW

♦**Step 7**   Using a drill press and a ½-inch-diameter drill with a ³⁄₁₆-inch deep setting, drill the 121 holes.

♦**Step 8**   Sand all over with fine-grit sandpaper. Apply a high-gloss coat of varnish.

♦**Step 9**   *Optional:* Glue a piece of felt cloth to the bottom surface and trim along its edge.

♦**Step 10**   Marbles or pegs can be used for pieces.

7 ♦ Toy Train

This is a classic toy (circa 1920). This train is still as popular today as it was in the 20s. Here is an old toy that is easy to make and takes very little wood. In fact, a ¾-inch-thick piece of wood 1½ inches wide and only 19 inches long is all that is needed for a complete train with hardly any waste. The wheels are made from a ⅞-inch-diameter dowel only 5 inches long.

Instructions

♦ **Step 1**   (Drawings are on the next page.) Cut a board ¾ inch thick, 1½ inches wide, and 19 inches long. Sand all over. Apply a light primer coat.

♦ **Step 2**   Carefully lay out the cars following the given dimensions. Cut out all of the cars and sand.

♦ **Step 3**   Cut the wheels from the ⅞-inch-diameter dowel into ¼-inch wide strips. Drill each wheel in the center for the axle.

♦ **Step 4**   Paint the cars and all of the wheels with nontoxic paint.

♦ **Step 5**   Add the wheels and eye screws. (Open every other eye screw to make a hook).

♦ **Step 6**   Optional: Sand all edges lightly, down to the bare wood. Apply a coat of light wood stain to create an original "antique" look. Watch the children's eyes light up when they see their new train.

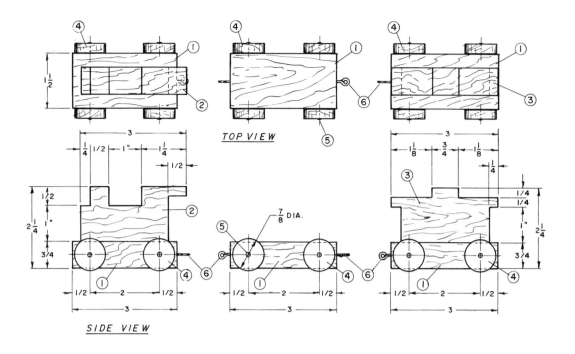

TOP VIEW

SIDE VIEW

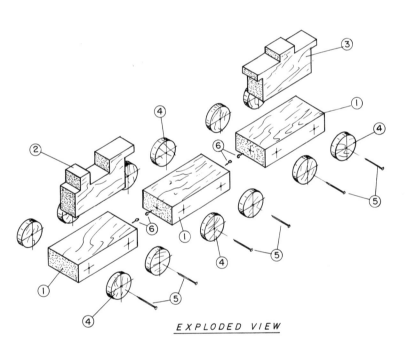

EXPLODED VIEW

NO.	NAME	SIZE	REQ'D.
1	BASE	3/4 X 1 1/2 - 3 LONG	4
2	ENGINE	3/4 X 1 1/2 - 3 LONG	1
3	CABOOSE	3/4 X 1 1/2 - 3 LONG	1
4	WHEEL	1/4 X 7/8 DIA.	16
5	AXLE	1" LONG TACK	16
6	EYESCREW	SMALL	6

MAKE FROM : ONE (1) 3/4 X 1 1/2 - 19 LONG
ONE (1) DOWEL -- 7/8 DIA. X 5 LONG

Note: There are actually four cars; make two cars from the middle car design. With a few eye screws, tacks, and paint, your train is ready to go!

8♦Four-Wheel Cars

Today the rage, at least in southern New Hampshire, is four-wheel-drive cars or off-road vehicles. I teach at a local high school, and Monday mornings all I hear about are stories of off-road trips. With this in mind, I thought the younger children would also be interested in their own 4-wheel-drive or off-road vehicle. Here are four popular models of today, the Amigo, Sidekick, Rocky, and the U.S.-made Jeep Wrangler.

You will need a scroll saw or band saw with a very thin blade in it for this project.

Instructions

♦**Step 1**   (Drawings are on the next page.) Transfer the shape of the pieces to the wood.

♦**Step 2**   Cut the *center* pieces first. Locate and drill the ⅛-inch-diameter holes for the axles.

♦**Step 3**   Tape or tack the two side pieces together. Cut both out at the same time so you will have a perfect pair.

♦**Step 4**   Glue the sides, parts number 1, to the center, part number 2, and sand all edges as needed. Round the top and sides slightly as the original vehicle would be rounded. Do *not* round the area where the fenders will be glued on.

♦**Step 5**   If needed, cut out the fenders, and glue them to the body.

♦**Step 6**   Temporarily add the wheels, parts number 4, and the axle pins, parts number 5. Check that you have clearance and that the wheels turn easily.

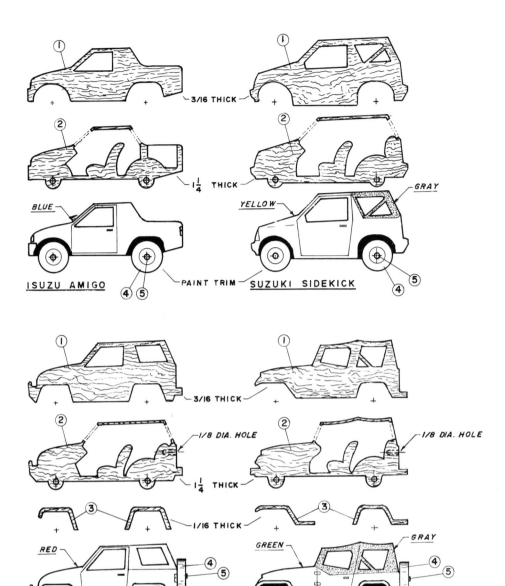

For each car :

NO.	NAME	SIZE	REQ'D.
1	SIDE	3/16 X 2 - 4 1/2 LONG	2
2	CENTER	1 1/4 X 2 - 4 1/2 LG.	1
3	FENDER	1/16 X 3/4 - 4 LONG	2
4	WHEEL 7/8 DIA.		4 - 5
5	AXLE PIN 1/8 DIA.		5 - 6

♦**Step 7**   Remove the wheels and paint the body to suit using bright shiny colors. Add accent colors for the top and bumpers.

♦**Step 8**   Paint the wheels and hubs.

♦**Step 9**   Assemble, and your cars are ready for fun and whatever off-road duty your children can put them through.

9 ◆ Turtle Footstool

Here is an interesting footstool that I saw at an outdoor flea market not long ago. It looked to be homemade. I didn't want to buy it, but the dealer didn't mind my taking a photo and a few overall measurements. So here is my version of that footstool. I would guess it was made in the 40s or so.

Instructions

◆ **Step 1** (The drawings are on the following three pages.) Cut all pieces to overall size.

◆ **Step 2** Transfer the shapes to the wood, and cut them out. Sand the edges as needed.

◆ **Step 3** Using a ⅛-inch-radius cove cutter with a ball-bearing follower, make the cut around the seat, part number 1.

◆ **Step 4** Assemble according to the drawing of the exploded view.

◆ **Step 5** Now here is where you can really show off your creative abilities. Your turtle can be realistic or "funky." It will brighten up any child's room. Watch it doesn't *snap* at you.

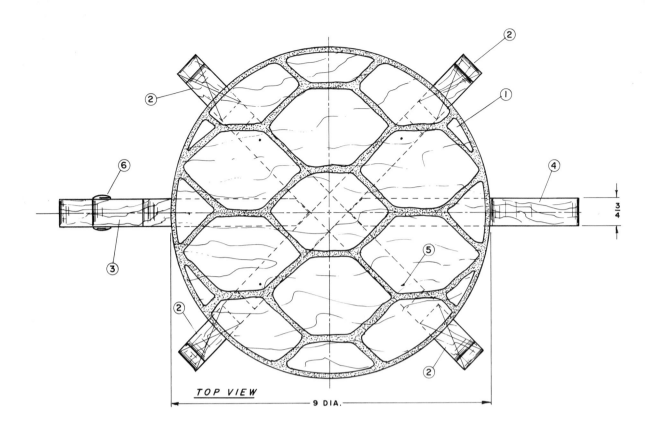

TOP VIEW

9 DIA.

3/4

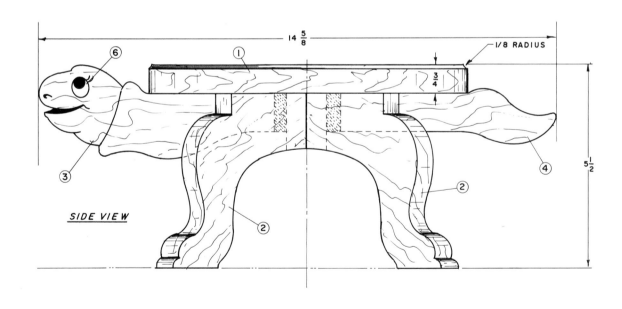

14 5/8

1/8 RADIUS

3/4

5 1/2

SIDE VIEW

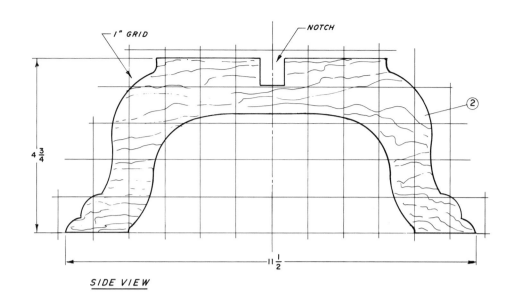

1" GRID

NOTCH

4 3/4

11 1/2

SIDE VIEW

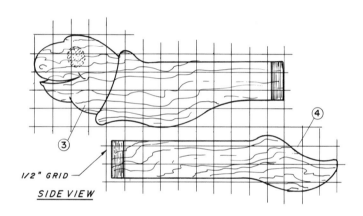

1/2" GRID

SIDE VIEW

NO.	NAME	SIZE	REQ'D.
1	SEAT	3/4 X 9 – 9 LONG	1
2	LEG	3/4 X 4 3/4 – 11 1/2	2
3	HEAD	3/4 X 2 1/2 – 7 LG.	1
4	TAIL	3/4 X 1 1/2 – 6 3/8	1
5	FINISH NAIL	6 d	12
6	EYE OVAL	5/8 SIZE	1 PR.

(Exploded view is on next page.)

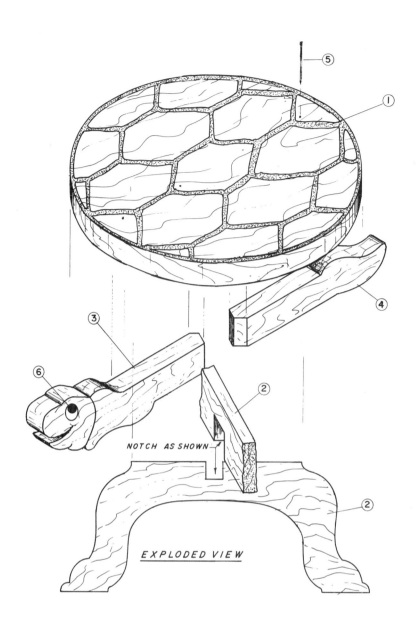

NOTCH AS SHOWN

EXPLODED VIEW

38

10 ◆ Toy Airplane

As a child growing up in Rhode Island next to the state airport in the early 40s, I can remember small biplanes, such as this one, taking off and landing. Even today, I can still hear their long-stroke engines "putting" along, overhead. It was a sound you just don't hear anymore. There is an aerodrome in Rhinebeck, New York, that still flies wonderful old airplanes, where you can hear that sound.

Instructions

◆ **Step 1** (The drawings are on the following three pages.) Glue up material to cut the body from. You should have a block of wood 2½ inches by 2½ inches that is 8⁵⁄₁₆ inches long.

◆ **Step 2** Using a band saw, cut out the airplane body, part number 1. Locate and drill all holes as noted. Round the edges as shown in the front view, section A–A, section B–B, and section C–C.

◆ **Step 3** Cut the two wings, parts number 2, to size as shown. Note that the *top* wing has a 1¾-inch radius cut out of it. Locate and drill the five ¼-inch-diameter holes.

◆ **Step 4** Make the remaining pieces according to the detail drawings.
Note: A lathe is needed to make the cowl, part number 6. Sand all over.

◆ **Step 5** Assemble all of the pieces following the drawing of the exploded view.

◆ **Step 6** Lightly sand, and paint to suit.

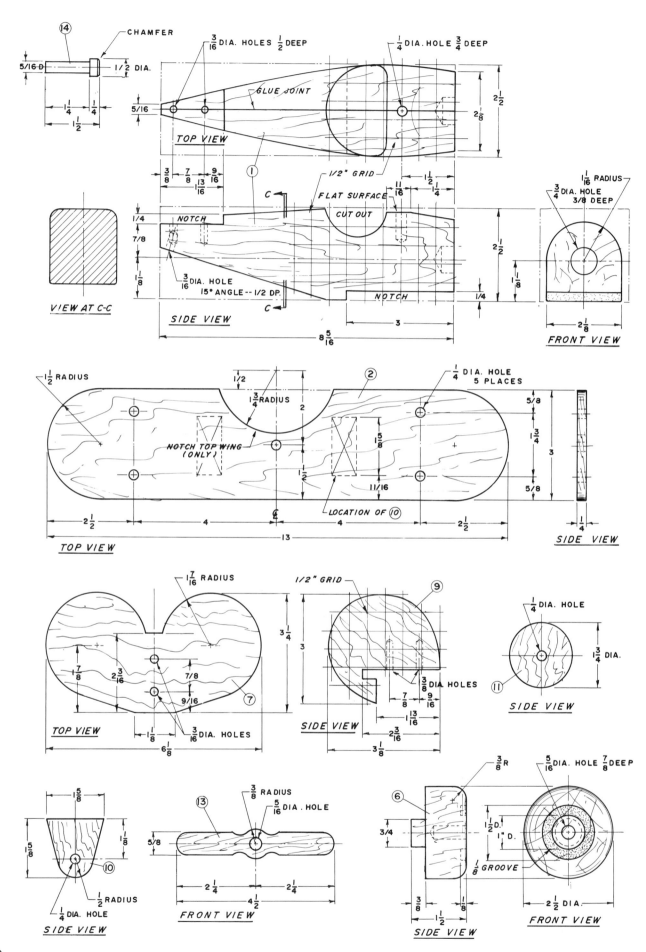

CHAMFER

⑭

5/16 D   1/2 DIA.

1/4   1/4
1 1/2

3/16 DIA. HOLES 1/2 DEEP

1/4 DIA. HOLE 3/4 DEEP

GLUE JOINT

5/16

2 1/8   2 1/2

TOP VIEW

①

3/8   7/8   9/16
1 13/16

1/2" GRID

FLAT SURFACE

CUT OUT

1 11/16   1 1/2   1 1/4

1 1/16 RADIUS

3/4 DIA. HOLE
3/8 DEEP

VIEW AT C-C

1/4

7/8

1 1/8

NOTCH

3/16 DIA. HOLE
15° ANGLE -- 1/2 DP.

C

C

2 1/2

NOTCH

1 1/8

1/4

3

SIDE VIEW

8 5/16

2 1/8

FRONT VIEW

1 1/2 RADIUS

1/2

1 3/4 RADIUS   2

②

NOTCH TOP WING
(ONLY)

1 5/8

1/2

1/4 DIA. HOLE
5 PLACES

5/8

1 3/4   3

5/8

2 1/2

4

€

LOCATION OF ⑩

11/16

4

2 1/2

1/4

TOP VIEW

13

SIDE VIEW

1 7/16 RADIUS

3 1/4

1/2" GRID

⑨

3

7/8

2 3/16

7/8

9/16

7

TOP VIEW

1 1/8

3/16 DIA. HOLES

6 1/8

3/16 DIA HOLES

7/8   9/16
1 13/16
2 3/16

SIDE VIEW

3 1/8

1/4 DIA. HOLE

1 3/4 DIA.

⑪

SIDE VIEW

1 5/8

5/8

1 1/8

⑩

1/2 RADIUS

1/4 DIA. HOLE

SIDE VIEW

⑬

3/8 RADIUS

5/16 DIA. HOLE

5/8

2 1/4   2 1/4
4 1/2

FRONT VIEW

3/8 R

5/16 DIA. HOLE 7/8 DEEP

⑥

3/4

1 1/2 D.

1" D.

1/8 GROOVE

3/8   1 1/2   1/8

SIDE VIEW

2 1/2 DIA.

FRONT VIEW

40

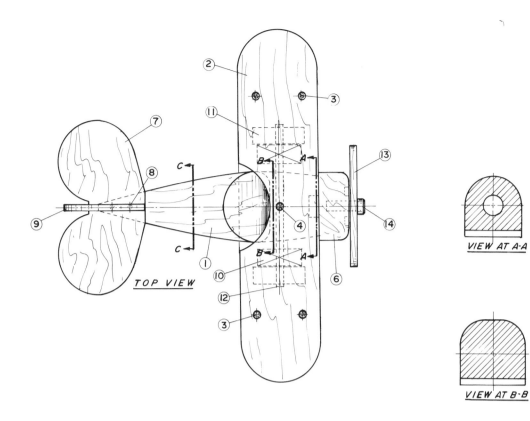

TOP VIEW

VIEW AT A-A

VIEW AT B-B

VIEW AT C-C

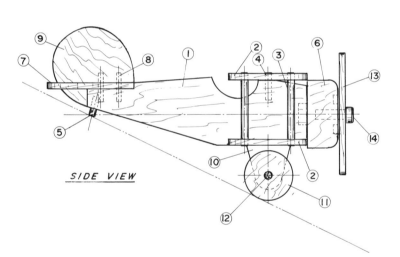

SIDE VIEW

(Exploded view is on next page.)

NO	NAME	SIZE	REQ'D.
1	BODY SIDE	1 1/4 X 2 1/2 – 8 5/16	2
2	WING	1/4 X 3 – 13 LONG	2
3	STRUT	1/4 DIA. X 2 3/4 LG.	4
4	PIN FOR WING	1/4 DIA. X 1" LG.	1
5	TAIL PIN	3/16 DIA. X 3/4 LG.	1
6	COWEL	2 1/2 DIA. X 1 1/2 LG.	1
7	ELEVATOR	1/4 X 3 1/4 – 6 1/8 LG.	1
8	PIN FOR RUDDER	3/16 DIA. X 1 1/2 LG.	2
9	RUDDER	1/4 X 3 – 3 1/2 LG.	1
10	SUPPORT	3/4 X 1 5/8 – 1 5/8	2
11	WHEEL	3/4 X 1 3/4 SQ.	2
12	AXLE	1/4 DIA. X 6 7/8 LG.	1
13	PROP	3/16 X 3/4 – 4 1/2	1
14	PEG	1/2 DIA. X 1 1/4 LG.	1

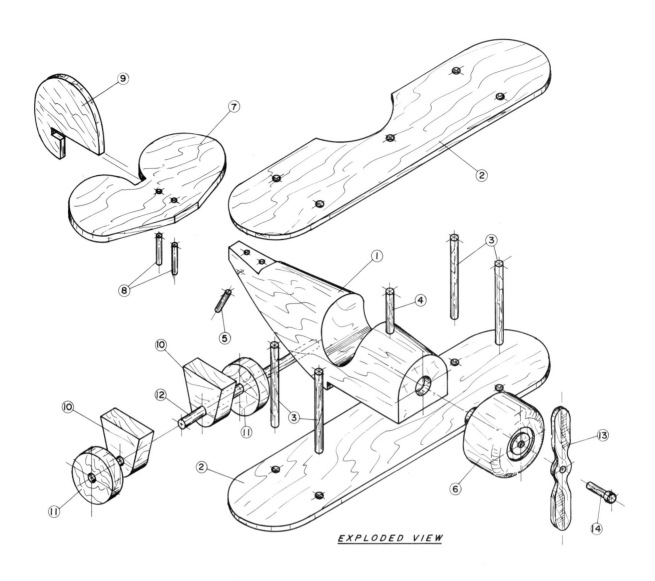

EXPLODED VIEW

11♦Pelican Pull Toy

I found this wonderful toy in an antique shop in northern New Hampshire. It was in great shape, so I just had to have it. I believe it was handmade by some loving father for his son or daughter and makes a great pull toy. As you can see, the pelican's mouth opens and closes as he "walks" along.

Instructions

♦**Step 1** (The drawings are on the following pages.) Study how the pelican is put together. It is important that you understand how it works before starting.

♦**Step 2** Cut all wood to overall size.

♦**Step 3** Transfer all shapes and details to the wood.

♦**Step 4** Carefully make the notch and step in the base, part number 7, and drill the required holes following the plans.

♦**Step 5** Cut and sand all other pieces according to the detailed drawings.

♦**Step 6** Bend the connecting rod, part number 15, and front axle, part number 12, as shown.

♦**Step 7** Glue the wings, parts number 2, to the body, part number 1.

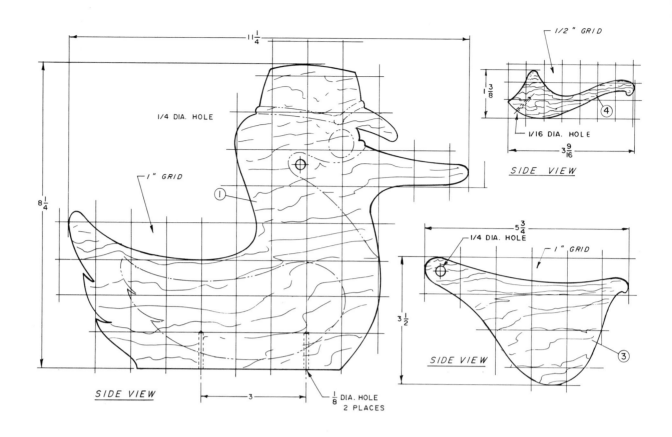

11 1/4

1/4 DIA. HOLE

1" GRID

8 1/4

1

SIDE VIEW

3

1/8 DIA. HOLE
2 PLACES

1/2 " GRID

1 3/8

4

1/16 DIA. HOLE

3 9/16

SIDE VIEW

5 3/4

1/4 DIA. HOLE

1" GRID

3 1/2

SIDE VIEW

3

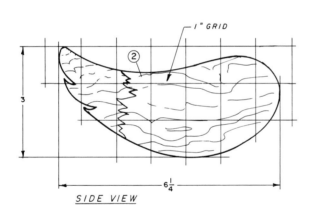

1" GRID

2

3

6 1/4

SIDE VIEW

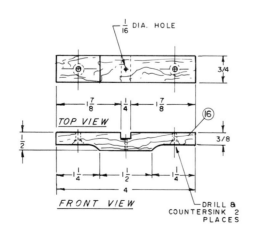

1/16 DIA. HOLE

3/4

1 7/8   1/4   1 7/8

TOP VIEW

16

1/2

3/8

1/4   1 1/2   1/4

4

FRONT VIEW

DRILL &
COUNTERSINK 2
PLACES

NO.	NAME	SIZE	REQ'D.
1	BODY	1/2 X 8 1/4 – 11 1/4	1
2	WING	1/4 X 3 – 6 1/4 LG.	2
3	BILL	1/4 X 3 1/2 – 5 3/4	2
4	FILLER	9/16 X 1 3/8 – 3 9/16	1
5	PIN	1/4 DIA. – 1 1/16 LG.	1
6	JIGGLE EYE	1" OVAL	1 PR.
7	BASE	3/4 X 4 – 7 1/2 LG.	1
8	SCREW -- FL. HD.	NO. 6 – 1 1/2 LG.	2
9	AXLE SUPPORT (R)	1/2 X 1 1/8 – 4 LG.	1
10	AXLE SUPPORT (F)	1/2 X 1 1/8 – 1 3/8	2
11	WHEEL	1/2 X 2 1/2 DIA.	4
12	FRONT AXLE	WIRE – 6 1/4 LONG	1
13	REAR AXLE	WIRE – 5 1/4 LONG	1
14	EYE-SCREW	SMALL SIZE	1
15	CONNECTING ROD	WIRE X 3 3/4 LG.	1
16	BUMPER	1/2 X 3/4 – 4 LONG	1
17	SCREW--FL. HD.	NO.6 – 3/4 LONG	2
18	EYE-SCREW	MEDIUM SIZE	1

44

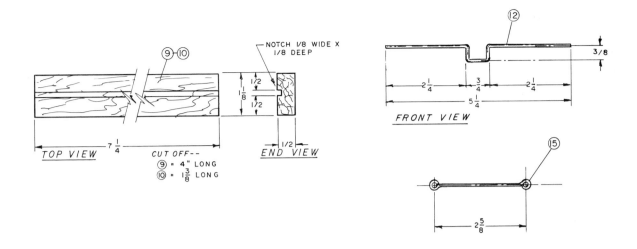

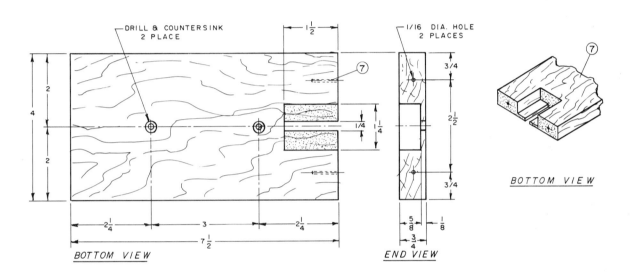

♦ **Step 8** Glue the filler, part number 4, to the bill, part number 3.

♦ **Step 9** *Temporarily* add the pin, part number 5; also check that everything moves smoothly and easily.

♦ **Step 10** Glue and screw the body, part number 1, to the base, part number 7, using the two screws, parts number 8.

♦ **Step 11** Glue the axle supports, parts number 9 and 10. Be sure to attach the connecting rod, part number 15, to the front axle, part number 12. Add the rod and front axle at *the same time* as the two front axle supports, parts number 10.

♦ **Step 12** Screw the bumper, part number 16, with the screws, parts number 17, to the base, part number 7.

♦ **Step 13** Connect the eye screw, part number 14, to the pelican's bill, part number 4, as shown, and attach the connecting rod, part number 15, to it. Check that everything moves correctly as the front axle turns. (Continued on the following two pages.)

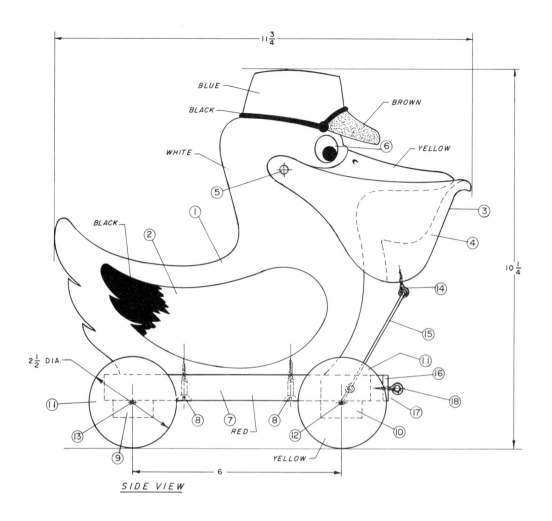

SIDE VIEW

♦**Step 14** Remove the pin, part number 5, and paint all pieces to suit. Make the pelican bright.

♦**Step 15** Add the eyes, parts number 6, and front eye screw, part number 18.

♦**Step 16** Reattach the bill assembly with the pin, part number 5.

♦**Step 17** Epoxy the wheels to the axles so that they will not come loose, but will still turn with the axles. Check that the bill moves as the front wheel turns.

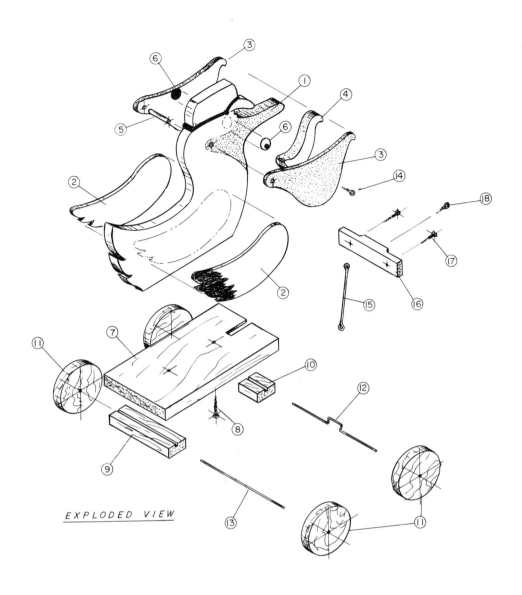

EXPLODED VIEW

♦ **Step 18** Add a pull string and your pelican is ready for a walk around the house.

FOLK ART

12 ◆ Door Stop

Here is a sleeping Mexican, another design I found in an antique shop. According to the shop owner, these were popular in the 30s and 40s. Today it still makes a great door stop and an even better conversation piece.

Instructions

◆ **Step 1**   Using a ½-inch grid, draw the pattern on a sheet of heavy paper.

◆ **Step 2**   Transfer the pattern to the wood.

◆ **Step 3**   Cut out and sand all edges.

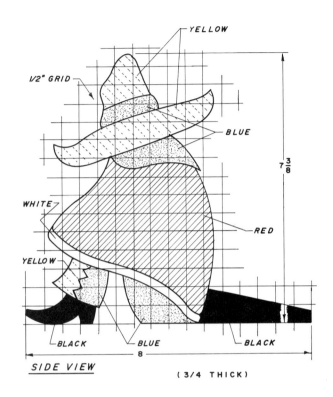

YELLOW

1/2" GRID

BLUE

7 3/8

WHITE

RED

YELLOW

BLACK   BLUE   BLACK

8

SIDE VIEW   (3/4 THICK)

♦**Step 4** Paint with bright colors. I distressed mine slightly and sanded the edges to make it look old and "original." If you want to really make it look old and worn, apply a coat of dark stain over the paint.

Sit back and watch the reactions of family and friends.

13♦Swan Decoration

Here is an interesting wall hanging. It should be made of old wood, preferably, or new wood that is distressed.

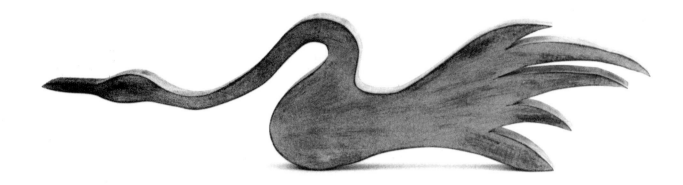

Instructions

♦**Step 1** Make a full-size pattern and apply it to the wood.

♦**Step 2** Cut out and sand all over.

♦**Step 3** Paint using an antique white paint, and sand the edges down to the bare wood.

♦**Step 4** Apply a coat of dark stain and wipe off excessive stain.

♦**Step 5** When the swan is dry, add a hanger and your swan is ready to be displayed.

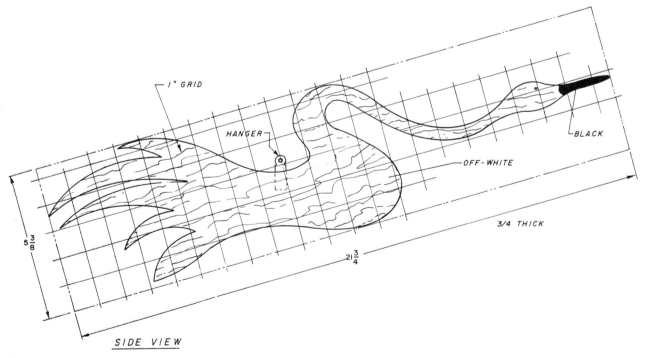

14 ♦ Weather Vanes

Weather vanes are as popular today as they were 100 years ago. Both of these patterns are taken directly from original weather vanes. You can distress these, if you want them to look old. Weather vanes have been used for centuries, perhaps even millennia. The rooster is an old symbol used to identify places of worship of the early church, since Peter made his three denials before the cock crowed. The arrow points into the wind and stays aligned as the wind changes. The cock weather vane on church steeples signified how easily faith could be swayed.

Instructions

♦ **Step 1**   (The patterns are on the following page.) Lay out either or both patterns on a ½-inch grid.

♦ **Step 2**   Transfer the pattern(s) to the wood and cut out.

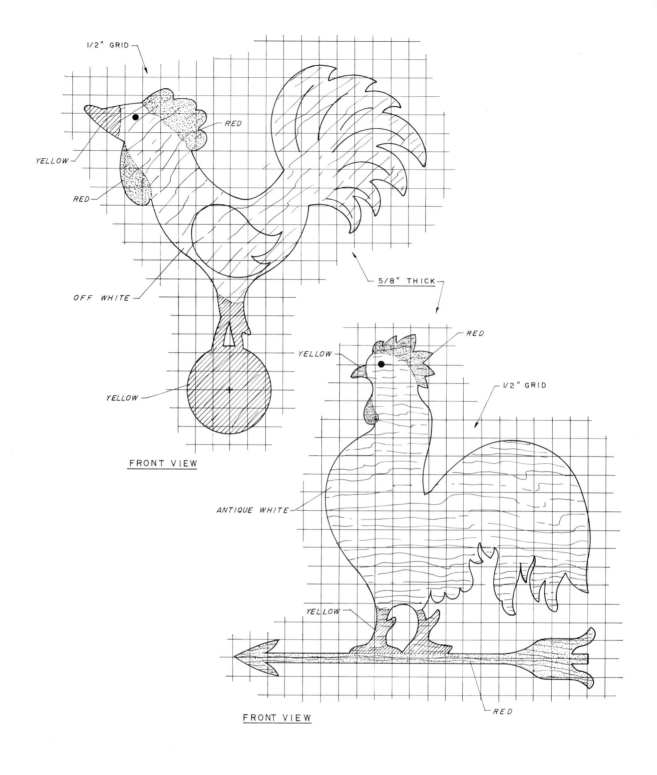

1/2" GRID

YELLOW

RED

RED

OFF WHITE

YELLOW

FRONT VIEW

5/8" THICK

YELLOW

RED

1/2" GRID

ANTIQUE WHITE

YELLOW

RED

FRONT VIEW

♦ **Step 3** Paint to suit. I prefer sanding the edges slightly and staining over the paint to get an old look.

These weather vanes make great wall hangings.

52

15 ◆ Plant Holder

A friend wanted a wall plant holder. She wanted "something different." Well, here it is. It is bright and different!

Instructions

◆**Step 1** (The drawings are on the following pages.) Lay out the patterns for parts number 1 and 2 on heavy paper.

◆**Step 2** Transfer the pattern to the wood, and cut out parts number 1 and 2. Sand all over.

◆**Step 3** Using a ⅛-inch-radius cove cutter with a ball-bearing follower cut the outer edge of the support, part number 1.

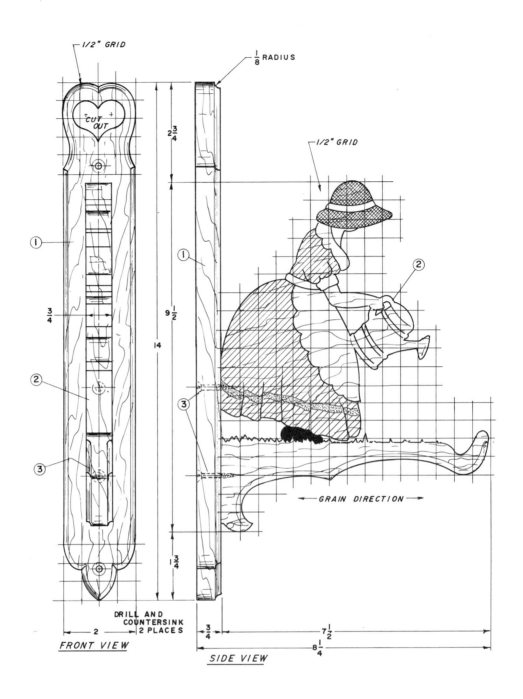

♦ **Step 4** Drill the holes in the support, part number 1.

♦ **Step 5** Glue and screw the body, part number 2, to the support, part number 1, using screws, parts number 3.

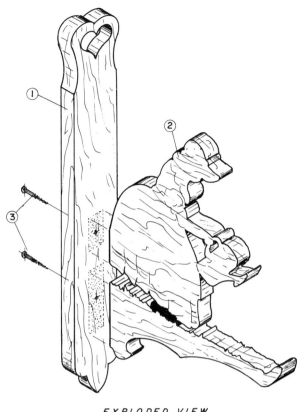

EXPLODED VIEW

NO.	NAME	SIZE	REQ'D.
1	SUPPORT	3/4 X 2 - 14 LONG	1
2	BODY	3/4 X 9 1/2 - 7 1/2 LG.	1
3	SCREW - FL. HD.	NO. 6 - 1 3/4 LONG	2

♦ **Step 6**   Prime and paint with bright colors, to suit. Hang on the wall, and add your favorite plant.

16 ◆ Scroll Saw Shelf

These small shelves come in many shapes and sizes. Many were made in the 30s so that they are now finding their way into antique shops. I found this one on Block Island (off Rhode Island). The original was a little rough, so I had to smooth out the lines a little.

Instructions

◆**Step 1**   Carefully make a full-size pattern.

◆**Step 2**   A trick I like to do in making fretwork projects is to *finish* the surfaces *before* cutting out the shape. Cut the wood to overall sizes and sand. Add a stain and two or three top-coats of varnish or shellac, sanding between coats.

   Note: Finish both sides.

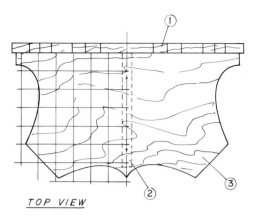

TOP VIEW

NO.	NAME	SIZE	REQ'D.
1	BACK	1/4 X 6 1/2 – 11 1/2 LG.	1
2	BRACE	1/4 X 3 5/16 – 4 13/16	1
3	SHELF	1/4 X 3 3/8 – 6 1/4 LG.	1
4	BRAD·	3/4 LONG	6

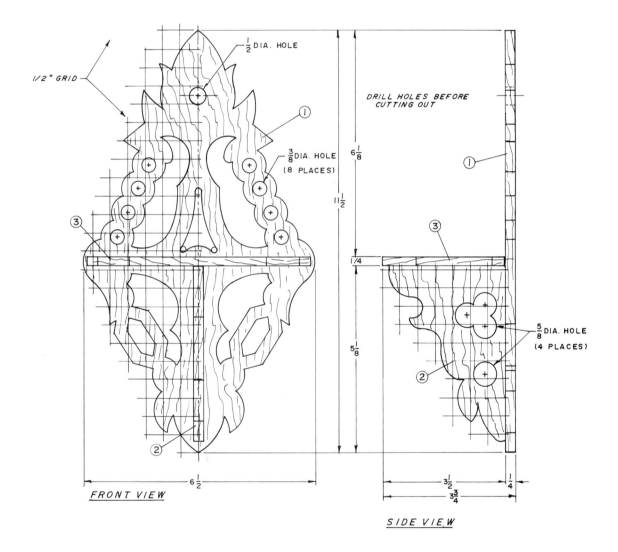

FRONT VIEW

SIDE VIEW

◆ **Step 3**   Glue the paper pattern to the wood, using a thin coat of rubber cement or a spray-mount adhesive. To get a smooth back surface, lightly glue a plain piece of paper to the back, also.

◆ **Step 4**   Locate and drill the eight ⅜-inch-diameter holes. Cut out the pattern.

◆ **Step 5**   Peel the paper pattern and back sheet from the wood and lightly sand. (Continued on next page.)

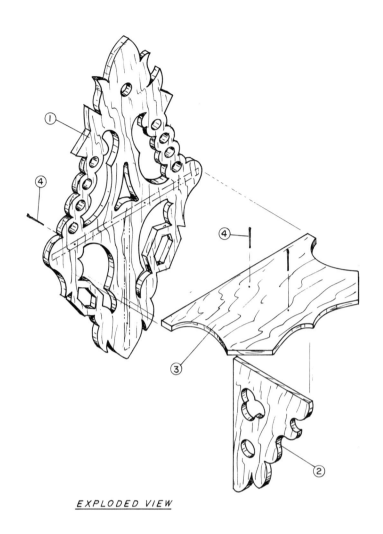

EXPLODED VIEW

♦**Step 6**   Assemble using small brads, predrilling all holes.

The shelf is ready to be used for the next 50 years.

17♦Parrot Wall Decoration

Now here is a bird I like! You don't have to feed it, you don't have to clean up after it, and it doesn't make any noise; my kind of bird!

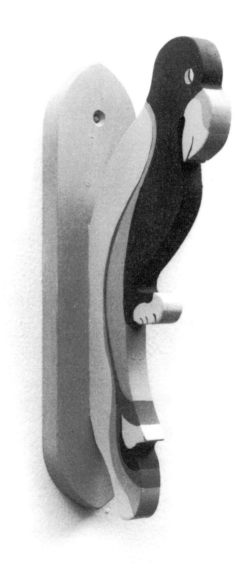

I found this bird in an antique shop in northern Massachusetts. No one knew what it was used for, but it had a very high price tag; so I guess it is a wonderful thing to have! From a few photographs and the overall dimensions, here it is! Do with it as you wish. I would guess it dates from the 30s or early 40s.

Instructions

♦**Step 1**   (The drawings are on the following page.) Make a full-size pattern and transfer it to the wood.

♦**Step 2**   Cut out both pieces, and sand all edges.

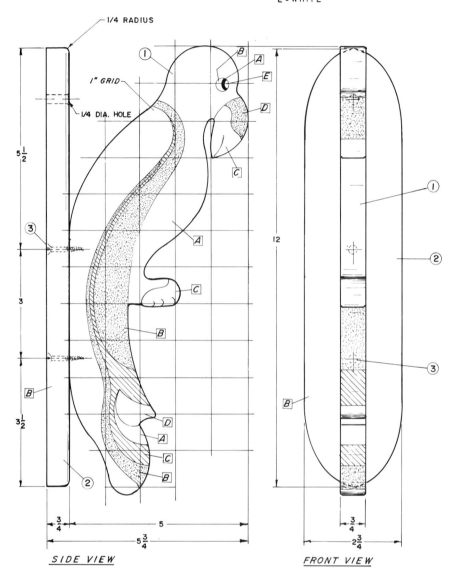

NO.	NAME	SIZE	REQ'D.
1	BODY	3/4 X 5 — 12 1/4 LG.	1
2	BRACKET	3/4 X 2 3/4 — 12 LG.	1
3	SCREW—FL.HD.	NO. 8 — 1 1/4 LONG	2

♦ **Step 3**   Screw the pieces together.

♦ **Step 4**   Prime and paint as you wish. If you want to copy the original exactly, then use the colors as noted.

18 ◆ Roadrunner

Like the weather vane, the whirligig is true American Folk Art. They once depicted all walks of life; performing chores of the day from chopping wood to milking cows. Made in all shapes and sizes, they featured spinning wings, propellers, waving arms, kicking legs, and presented just about every motif imaginable.

This one is a copy of one I found in an antique shop in northern New Hampshire. The original may be only thirty-five years old, since I don't think the roadrunner design was around before then.

The metal parts required for this project are the same as for any whirligig and can be ordered from mail-order suppliers. The little extra spent on brass parts is well worth it, especially since the wood parts can be made from scrap. Use a straight grain, knot-free hardwood, waterproof glue, and exterior primer and paint. (Instructions and drawings are on following pages.)

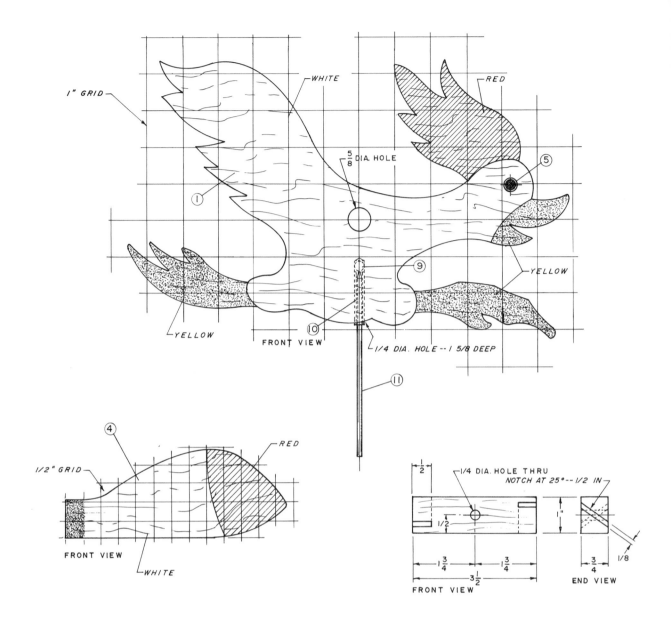

Instructions

♦ **Step 1** Using a 1-inch grid for the body and a ½-inch grid for the wing, lay out the full-size pattern.

♦ **Step 2** Cut all wood to size according to the materials list.

♦ **Step 3** Transfer the body pattern and hole locations to the wood, and cut out the shape. A band saw is best, but a jigsaw or even a coping saw will work fine. After all, the original was made without any power tools. Drill a ⅝-inch-diameter hole for the wing support and a ¼-inch-diameter hole in the underside edge as shown on the drawing.

♦ **Step 4** Cut the wing support from a ⅝-inch-diameter dowel, and glue it to the body. Locate the exact center of each end of the dowel, and drill pilot holes for the wood screws.

♦ **Step 5** Drill a ¼-inch-diameter hole in each hub (D). Kerf one end of each; then kerf the other end, but in opposite positions as shown. The flat edges of the wings face in the same general direction and are located on the same side of the hub.

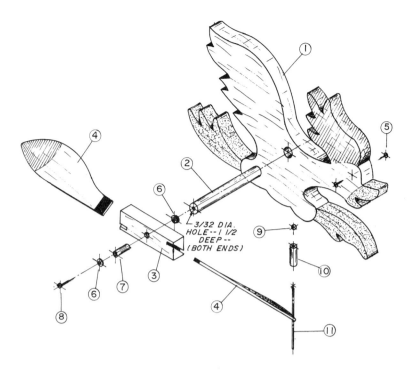

EXPLODED VIEW

NO.	NAME	SIZE	REQ'D.
1	BODY	3/4 X 7 5/8 - 13 LG.	1
2	WING SUPPORT	5/8 DIA. - 4 1/4 LG.	1
3	CENTER HUB	3/4 X 1 - 3 1/2 LG.	2
4	WING	1/8 X 2 1/2 - 6 1/2	4
5	EYE 1/2 DIA.		2
6	WASHER 7/16 DIA.		4
7	TUBE		2
8	SCREW - RD. HEAD		2
9	PIVOT BEARING		1
10	PIVOT TUBE		1
11	PIVOT NAIL		1

♦Step 6   Prime the wood with exterior primer; then paint with exterior paint—any color combination will look good, but I suggest bright colors. When dry, assemble the project as shown in the exploded view. The wings must turn freely, so don't over-tighten the wing screws. The pivot bearing, a brass or steel ball, is held in place by the pivot tube. Attach the eyes and your bird is done.

19♦Cat Night Stand

Now this is a Folk Art project right out of the 30s. This was actually used for a smoking stand to support an ashtray. As a kid, I can remember them. I have seen more and more of these smoking stands in local antique shops. They are becoming collectibles. I decided not to call this a smoking stand, since people are supposedly trying to quit the smoking habit.

Instructions

♦**Step 1**   Make a full-size pattern of the body, part number 1.

♦**Step 2**   Cut all pieces to overall size and sand.

♦**Step 3**   Transfer the pattern of the body, part number 1, to the wood, and cut out. Sand all edges slightly.

♦**Step 4**   Cut the base, part number 2, and two supports, parts number 3 and 4, to shape and sand all over.

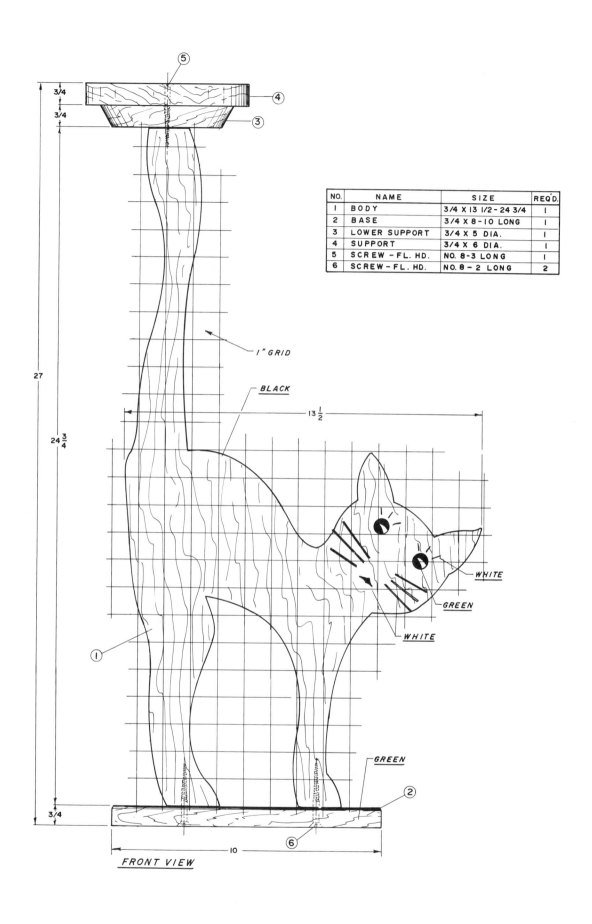

NO.	NAME	SIZE	REQ'D.
1	BODY	3/4 X 13 1/2 - 24 3/4	1
2	BASE	3/4 X 8 - 10 LONG	1
3	LOWER SUPPORT	3/4 X 5 DIA.	1
4	SUPPORT	3/4 X 6 DIA.	1
5	SCREW – FL. HD.	NO. 8 - 3 LONG	1
6	SCREW – FL. HD.	NO. 8 - 2 LONG	2

FRONT VIEW

♦ **Step 5** Drill for the screws, parts number 5 and 6. (Continued on next page.)

EXPLODED VIEW

◆**Step 6** Assemble the pieces according to the drawing of the exploded view.

◆**Step 7** Prime and paint to suit. Now your stand is all ready to use.

20 ◆ Lawn Bird, circa 1935

As a young boy growing up in Rhode Island in the early 40s, I can remember seeing these crazy birds all over. It seems every street had at least one of these birds with its head bobbing in the wind. By the time I was a teenager, they had all disappeared.

For years I had been looking for one so I could make my own. I finally found one in an antique shop in southern Connecticut, but it was just too expensive and the shop owner wouldn't let me photograph or measure it. A couple of years later I found another in northern Vermont. I was able to make a pattern from it, and I made a couple of them and have one on my front lawn right now—I think.

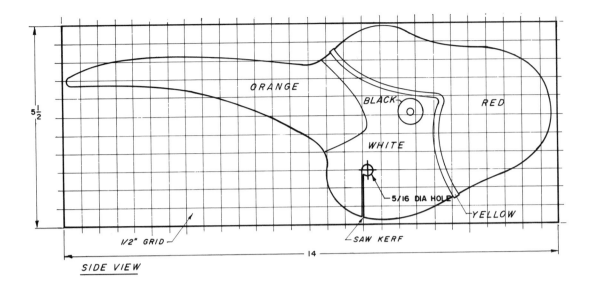

ORANGE BLACK RED WHITE YELLOW

5½   14

1/2" GRID   5/16 DIA HOLE   SAW KERF

SIDE VIEW

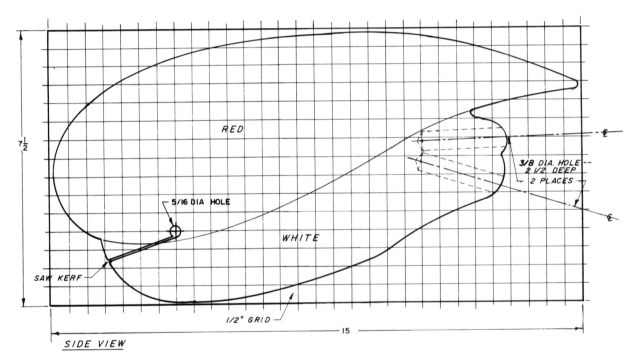

RED   WHITE

7½   15

5/16 DIA HOLE   3/8 DIA. HOLE 2 1/2 DEEP 2 PLACES

SAW KERF   1/2" GRID

SIDE VIEW

My bird disappears for three or four days at a time; but then it all of a sudden returns, as mysteriously as it left. It makes for a lot of fun and is a great conversation piece. If anyone knows about where these birds originally came from and why, I would love to know more about them.

Instructions

◆ **Step 1** Make up a full-size pattern, and cut out the head and body. Sand all edges. Don't forget to make a saw kerf for the spring.

◆ **Step 2** Locate and drill the two ⅜-inch-diameter holes for the legs and the ⁵⁄₁₆-inch-diameter holes for the spring.

◆ **Step 3** The spring can be purchased from a supplier or from a clock repair shop. It is part of a 30-day spring-driven clock. Keep the neck as long as possible so it just supports the head. The head should bob in a gentle wind.

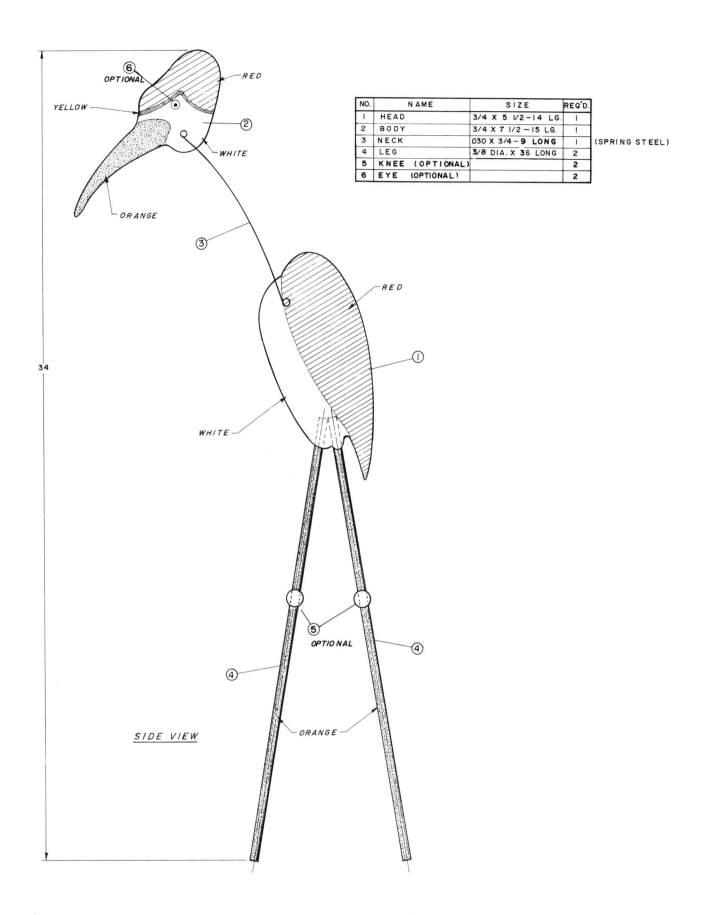

NO.	NAME	SIZE	REQ'D.
1	HEAD	3/4 X 5 1/2 - 14 LG.	1
2	BODY	3/4 X 7 1/2 - 15 LG.	1
3	NECK	.030 X 3/4 - 9 LONG	1	(SPRING STEEL)
4	LEG	3/8 DIA. X 36 LONG	2
5	KNEE (OPTIONAL)		2
6	EYE (OPTIONAL)		2

SIDE VIEW

♦ **Step 4** Prime and paint your bird; color as you wish. I used red and white but any color combination should upset your neighbors. (No pink birds, please!) Be sure to use exterior paint.

21 ♦ Paperweight

This is an interesting project that can be used as a paperweight or simply a conversation piece. If you have a 1-inch and 2-inch-diameter Forstner bit, and a ½-inch-diameter drill, it's very simple. It's a project that no one can leave alone. Put it on your desk and watch how everyone picks it up—they'll wonder how you made it.

Instructions

♦ **Step 1**   Start with a solid 2½-inch cube. If you have a solid piece of wood large enough, use it. If not, glue together scraps slightly larger than the 2½ inches needed—that's what I did with scrap pieces of ash. You might want to make two or three blocks to start with in case you set a drill depth incorrectly later on.

The only tricky part of the project is that your block must be *exactly* 2½ inches on all sides, and it must be square. If not, then the rest of the steps will not come out correctly. Sand all six surfaces using a sanding block, keeping all edges sharp.

♦ **Step 2**   Using a sharp pencil, draw light diagonal lines from corner to corner, as shown in the drawing, to locate the exact center of each surface. Using a pointed punch, prick-punch the exact center of each surface.

♦ **Step 3**   The drilling must be done on a drill press with an adjustable depth stop. With a 2-inch-diameter Forstner bit, drill a $^{15}/_{32}$-inch-deep hole in the center of all six surfaces. If your work has been precise, you should end up with a new block inside the outer block, hanging on by its corners, as shown in the drawings.

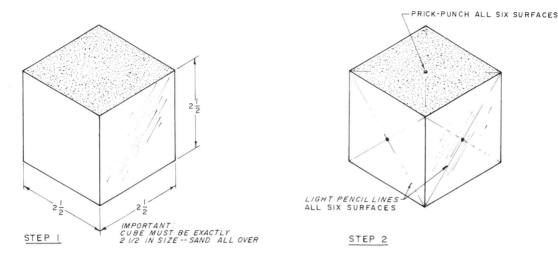

STEP I

IMPORTANT:
CUBE MUST BE EXACTLY
2 1/2 IN SIZE -- SAND ALL OVER

2½

2½   2½

PRICK-PUNCH ALL SIX SURFACES

LIGHT PENCIL LINES
ALL SIX SURFACES

STEP 2

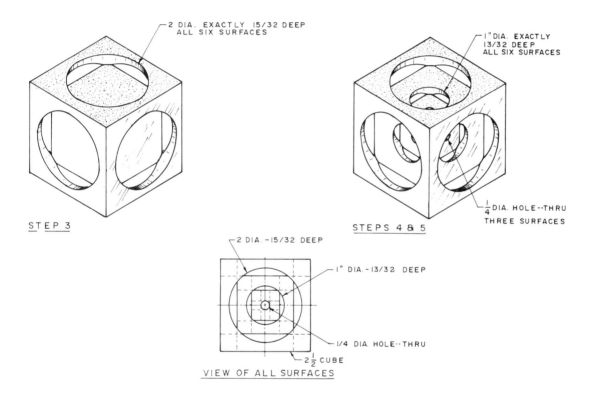

2 DIA. EXACTLY 15/32 DEEP
ALL SIX SURFACES

STEP 3

I" DIA. EXACTLY
13/32 DEEP
ALL SIX SURFACES

¼ DIA. HOLE--THRU
THREE SURFACES

STEPS 4 & 5

2 DIA. -15/32 DEEP

I" DIA. -13/32 DEEP

1/4 DIA. HOLE--THRU

2½ CUBE

VIEW OF ALL SURFACES

♦ **Step 4** Using the indent left by the tip of the 2-inch-diameter bit, drill a 1-inch-diameter hole exactly $^{13}/_{16}$ inches deep using a Forstner bit, centered inside each of the six 2-inch-diameter holes. The depth must be exact. You will find that you have created another block inside the two outer blocks.

♦ **Step 5** Finish up by drilling a ¼-inch-diameter hole in the indent left by the tip of the 1-inch-diameter bit.

If the wood grain is interesting, leave the cube unfinished. If you like color, interesting patterns can be achieved by painting the blocks or their side surfaces different colors.

Now leave it on your desk or any place where people are; watch how they can't resist picking it up. Most will think you carved out the inner blocks, and they will never realize how easy it really was to make—unless you tell them.

22 ♦ Christmas Tree Decoration

Here is a simple decoration that is easy to make and will add a festive flair to any setting. This makes a great craft fair project.

Instructions

♦**Step 1** Using a ¾-inch thick board 7½ inches wide and 16 inches long, lay out all pieces. If you plan to make a few of these, make a pattern of each part out of heavy cardboard or hardboard.

♦**Step 2** Locate and drill all ¼-inch-diameter holes. Do *not* drill through the base, part number 1.

♦**Step 3** Cut out all of the pieces, and sand all over. Round all edges slightly.

♦**Step 4** Glue the base, part number 1, to the center stem, part number 9.

♦**Step 5** Drill a ¼-inch-diameter hole into the star, part number 10, as shown.
  You might want to use a clamp to hold the star while drilling the hole. Do *not* drill through.

♦**Step 6** Assemble all parts and paint to suit.

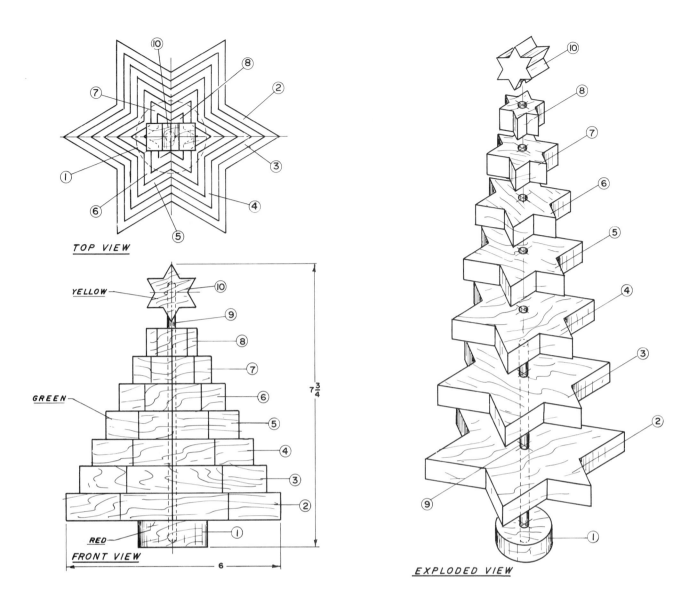

TOP VIEW

YELLOW

GREEN

RED

FRONT VIEW

6

7¾

EXPLODED VIEW

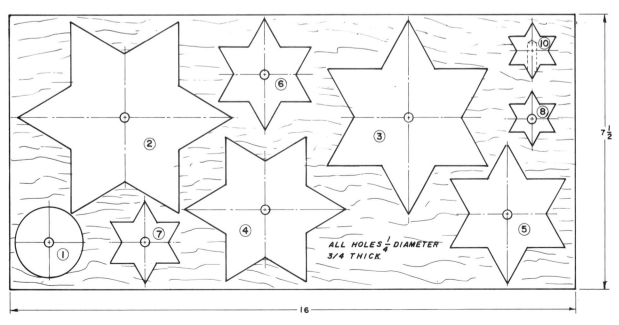

ALL HOLES ¼ DIAMETER
3/4 THICK

7½

16

73

HOUSEHOLD PROJECTS

23♦Rabbit Cutting Board

I have a very good friend, Jerry, whose wife, Pearl, *loves* rabbits. (Evidently she has never had to clean out a rabbit hutch!) She was always after her husband to make a rabbit cutting board. Not long ago when they were visiting with Joyce and myself, we were still unable to find a good pattern; so we decided to design our own. It was a bit hectic at first, as each of us knew what a rabbit should look like, but we all had different ideas. After a lot of drawing, and redrawing, we finally agreed on this design. It has a little of each of the ideas of the four of us in it. Hope you like it. Be sure to use a really pleasing hardwood for yours. The one in the photograph is made of ash.

Instructions

♦**Step 1**   Draw the full-size pattern using a ½-inch grid on a piece of heavy paper.

♦**Step 2**   Transfer the pattern to a good-looking piece of *hardwood*; ash, oak, maple are some suggestions.

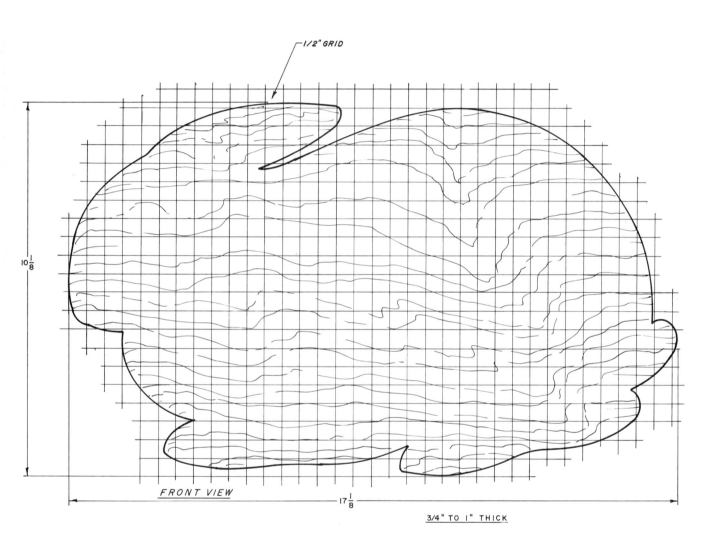

FRONT VIEW

1/2" GRID

10 $\frac{1}{8}$

17 $\frac{1}{8}$

3/4" TO 1" THICK

♦**Step 3** Cut out and sand.

♦**Step 4** Apply a coat of a nontoxic, clear oil.

24 ◆ Folding Candle Holder

While visiting a crafts shop during a recent summer, I saw a simple candle holder similar to this one. I found it very interesting. If you have a band saw it is very easy to make, although it can be made with a handsaw. It could be said this light has six candle power.

Instructions

◆ **Step 1**   Select a board with a pleasing grain pattern, preferably hardwood, and cut part number 1 to ¾ inches by 2⅞ inches by 8½ inches long.

◆ **Step 2**   Sand all over with coarse sandpaper down to a fine grit. Apply a coat of stain and one light top-coat. Lightly sand.

◆ **Step 3**   Locate and drill a ¼-inch-diameter hole through, at the right end, as shown.

◆ **Step 4**   Carefully locate and drill the six ½-inch-diameter holes 9/16 of an inch deep, as shown. Lightly resand.

◆ **Step 5**   Being precise and using a small square, draw the cuts on the side of the wood.

◆ **Step 6**   With great care, make the cuts as shown. Sand all fresh cuts and stain all surfaces again.

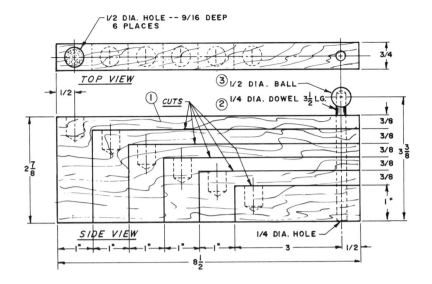

1/2 DIA. HOLE -- 9/16 DEEP
6 PLACES

TOP VIEW

3/4

1/2

① *CUTS*

③ 1/2 DIA. BALL

② 1/4 DIA. DOWEL 3½ LG.

2⅞

3/8
3/8
3/8
3/8
3/8

3⅜

1"

SIDE VIEW

1/4 DIA. HOLE

1" 1" 1" 1" 1" 3 1/2

8½

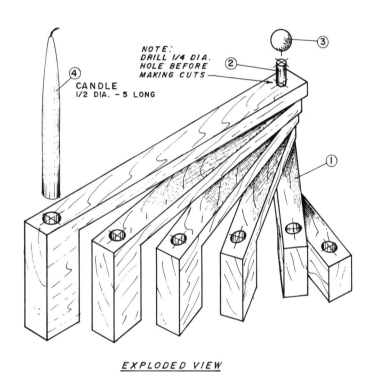

NOTE:
DRILL 1/4 DIA.
HOLE BEFORE
MAKING CUTS

③
②
①

④
CANDLE
1/2 DIA. – 5 LONG

EXPLODED VIEW

♦**Step 7**   Apply two to three more top-coats of a high-gloss finish.

♦**Step 8**   Temporarily add the ¼-inch-diameter dowel, part number 2, with a ½-inch-diameter ball, part number 3, on top.

♦**Step 9**   Fan out the fingers to check that the pieces clear each other. Trim lightly, as necessary.

♦**Step 10**   Attach the dowel again, part number 2, and ball, part number 3. Glue to the bottom board only. Add candles and open out the fingers in a fan-like position. Now all you need is a power failure to try out your candle holder.

25 ◆ Picture Frame

This is the design of a good friend of mine. It is very easy to make, attractive, and truly functional.

Instructions

◆**Step 1**   Cut all pieces to overall size.

◆**Step 2**   Cut the ends, parts number 1, to shape. Locate and drill the three $3/16$-inch-diameter holes. Do not drill through; drill only $3/16$ of an inch deep. Make the $3/16$-inch wide by $1/8$-inch deep dado. The width should be the width of two pieces of glass, plus a photo. Be sure to make a right-hand and a left-hand pair.

◆**Step 3**   Cut the three dowels, parts number 2, to length.

◆**Step 4**   Carefully glue the ends, parts number 1, to the three dowels, parts number 2. It is a good idea to have the glass temporarily in place so that the ends will be square.

◆**Step 5**   Add the small stops, parts number 3, as shown.

◆**Step 6**   Remove the glass; finish to suit. Add clean glass and a photo; now you have a beautiful, modern picture stand.

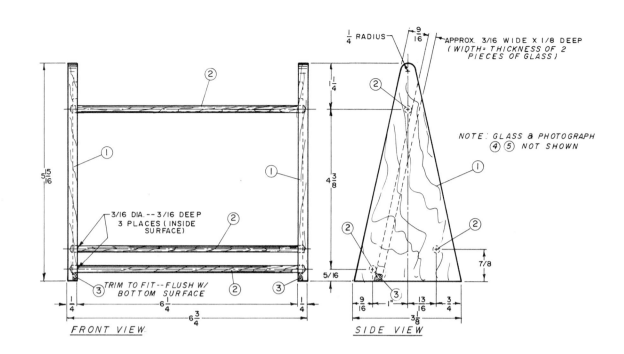

¼ RADIUS

APPROX. 3/16 WIDE X 1/8 DEEP
(WIDTH= THICKNESS OF 2
PIECES OF GLASS)

NOTE: GLASS & PHOTOGRAPH
④ ⑤ NOT SHOWN

3/16 DIA.--3/16 DEEP
3 PLACES (INSIDE
SURFACE)

TRIM TO FIT--FLUSH W/
BOTTOM SURFACE

FRONT VIEW

SIDE VIEW

NO.	NAME	SIZE	REQ'D.
1	END	1/4 X 3 1/8–6 LONG	2
2	DOWEL	3/16 DIA. –6 1/2 LG.	3
3	STOP	1/8 X 3/16 –3/16 LG.	2
4	GLASS	3/32 X 4 3/4–6 1/2	2
5	PHOTOGRAPH	4 3/4 X 6 1/2 SIZE	1

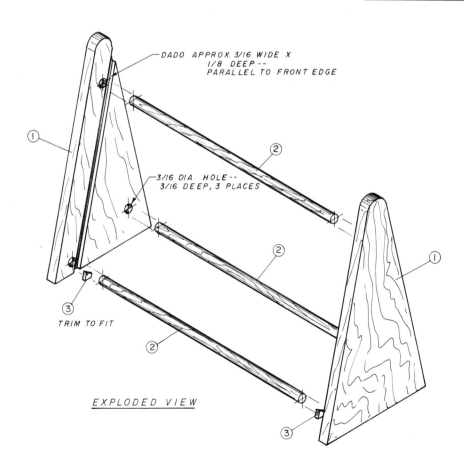

DADO APPROX. 3/16 WIDE X
1/8 DEEP --
PARALLEL TO FRONT EDGE

3/16 DIA. HOLE --
3/16 DEEP, 3 PLACES

TRIM TO FIT

EXPLODED VIEW

26 ◆ Folding Plant Stand

My wife, Joyce, has lots of plants but limited space to display them. I built this folding plant stand to give her room to pack more plants into a small area. It raises some plants above others and is a nice furniture piece.

Instructions

◆**Step 1**   Study the plans carefully before starting, so that you know how the legs fold together. Note the notch in the support, part number 3, to lock the legs in an open position.

◆**Step 2**   Cut the top pieces, parts number 1 and 2, to rough size. I suggest that you cut the pieces a little long.

◆**Step 3**   Cut the two supports, parts number 3, to size, and make the notch following detail "A." Drill a $\frac{1}{16}$-inch-diameter location hole in the opposite end for the screw, part number 8.

◆**Step 4**   Glue and tack the top pieces, parts number 1 and 2, to the two supports, parts number 3. Leave a $\frac{1}{4}$-inch space between parts. Be sure they are $2\frac{3}{4}$ inches apart and parallel, as shown.

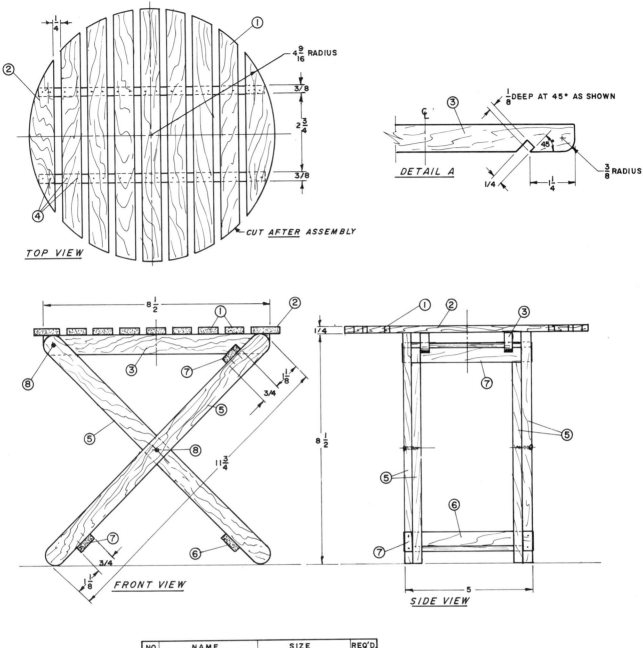

NO.	NAME	SIZE	REQ'D.
1	TOP-CENTER	1/4 X 3/4 – 9 1/4 LG.	7
2	TOP-END	1/4 X 1" – 9 1/4 LG.	2
3	SUPPORT	3/8 X 3/4 – 8 1/2 LG.	2
4	BRAD	5/8 LONG	48
5	LEG	3/8 X 3/4 – 11 3/4 LG.	4
6	BRACE	1/4 X 3/4 – 4 1/4 LG.	1
7	BRACE	1/4 X 3/4 – 5 1/16 LG.	2
8	SCREW – FL. HD.	NO. 6 – 5/8 LONG	4

♦**Step 5**   Locate the exact center of the top assembly and swing a 4⁹⁄₁₆-inch radius all of the way around. Sand down to the line so you have an exactly round top with all of the pieces in place.

♦**Step 6**   Carefully locate and drill a ¹⁄₁₆-inch-diameter hole for the screw, part number 8, at the crossover midpoint of the leg. (Continued on next page.)

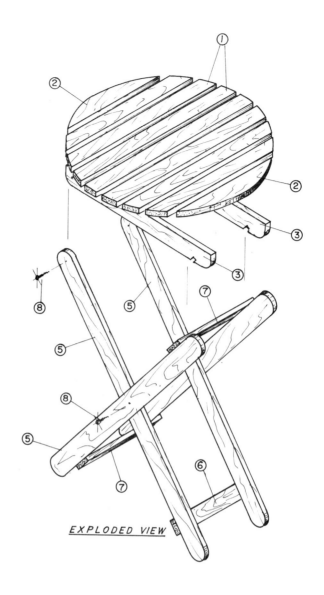

EXPLODED VIEW

♦**Step 7** Assemble all of the parts, and check that everything functions correctly. Check that the legs lock in an open position.

♦**Step 8** Finish to suit with either paint or stain.

27 ♦ Rabbit Plant Holder

Now here is a plant holder that is different! Usually, you want to keep the rabbits away from your plants. This one will attract a lot of attention.

Instructions

♦ **Step 1**   (The drawings are on the following page.) On a 1-inch grid lay out the profile of the side, part number 1.

♦ **Step 2**   Tack or tape two pieces of wood together. Transfer the profile to the wood, and cut both sides at the same time. Sand all edges. Cut the shelf, part number 2, to size, and drill two or three holes to fit your potted plants. Sand all over to remove all sharp edges.

♦ **Step 3**   Glue and nail together.

♦ **Step 4**   Paint to suit, but don't make it too realistic; you might attract *real* rabbits.

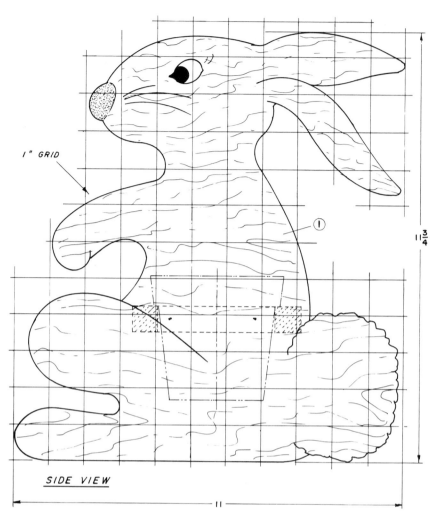

1" GRID

SIDE VIEW

①

11¾

11

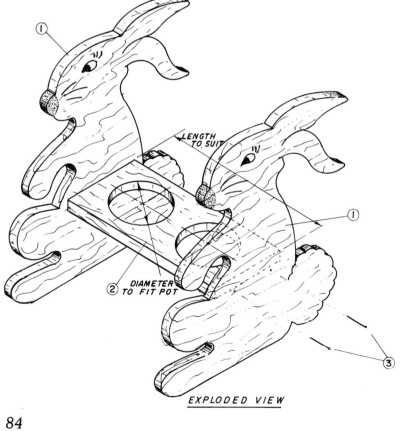

①

LENGTH TO SUIT

② DIAMETER TO FIT POT

①

③

EXPLODED VIEW

NO.	NAME	SIZE	REQ'D.
1	SIDE	1/2 X 11 3/4 – 11 LG.	2
2	SHELF	3/4 X 4 3/4 – LENGTH	1
3	FINISH NAIL	8 d	4

84

28 ◆ Knickknack Shelf

This what-not shelf provides a great place to display a small collection of your small collectibles. It looks great either painted or stained.

Instructions

◆**Step 1** (The drawings are on the following pages.) Cut all pieces to overall sizes and sand all surfaces.

◆**Step 2** Lay out and cut the back, part number 1, according to the given dimensions.

◆**Step 3** Carefully lay out and cut the three hearts in part number 2 following the given dimensions.

◆**Step 4** Dry-fit all of the pieces. If the pieces fit correctly, nail together as shown in the drawings.

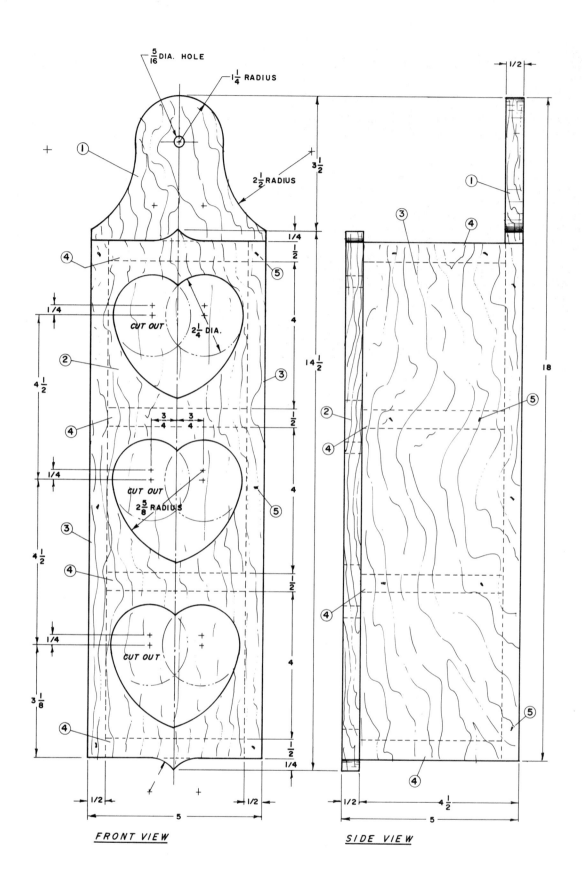

$\frac{5}{16}$ DIA. HOLE

$1\frac{1}{4}$ RADIUS

① ④ ②

CUT OUT $2\frac{1}{4}$ DIA.

CUT OUT $2\frac{5}{8}$ RADIUS

CUT OUT

$2\frac{1}{2}$ RADIUS

$3\frac{1}{2}$

$1/4$
$\frac{1}{2}$
⑤

$1/4$

$4\frac{1}{2}$

③

$14\frac{1}{2}$

4

$\frac{1}{2}$

$\frac{3}{4}$ $\frac{3}{4}$

④

$1/4$

⑤

4

$\frac{1}{2}$

$4\frac{1}{2}$

④

$1/4$

$3\frac{1}{8}$

4

④

$\frac{1}{2}$

$1/4$

$1/2$ $1/2$

5

FRONT VIEW

$1/2$

③ ④

①

⑤

④

⑤

④

$1/2$ $4\frac{1}{2}$

5

18

SIDE VIEW

86

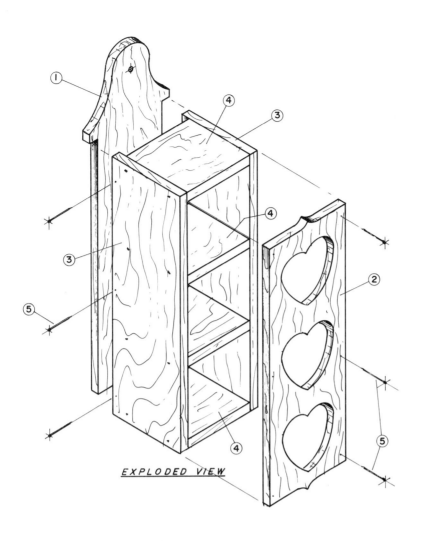

EXPLODED VIEW

NO.	NAME	SIZE	REQ'D.
1	BACK	1/2 X 5 - 18 LONG	1
2	FRONT	1/2 X 5 -14 1/2 LG.	1
3	SIDE	1/2 X 4 1/2 - 14 1/2	2
4	SHELF	1/2 X 4 - 4 LONG	4
5	FINISH NAIL	6 d	22

◆ **Step 5**   Sand all over. Round all of the edges slightly.

◆ **Step 6**   Paint or prime to suit.

29♦Bird House

I have designed and built many bird houses. This is the most elaborate one I have made. It is a takeoff of a Victorian house. I designed it based on an earlier, somewhat plain-Jane bird house of mine combined with one I saw in a magazine. This is a simple project, but it will require a little "fitting."

Instructions

♦**Step 1**   Cut all parts to overall size. It is a good idea to cut the front and back, parts number 1, to shape while the parts are either tacked or taped together, to insure an exact pair. (Only the *front* will have the 1¼-inch-diameter hole).

♦**Step 2**   Assemble the front, back, two sides, bottom, roof, and perch, parts number 1,2,3,4, and 5.
   Note: If you glue it together, use waterproof glue.

♦**Step 3**   Carefully add the trim as shown in the drawings. Add them in the order they are listed, that is, 6th first, 7th second, 8th third, etc. Glue and use small headless brads for the trim. Test if your wood tends to split. If so, predrill for the nails.

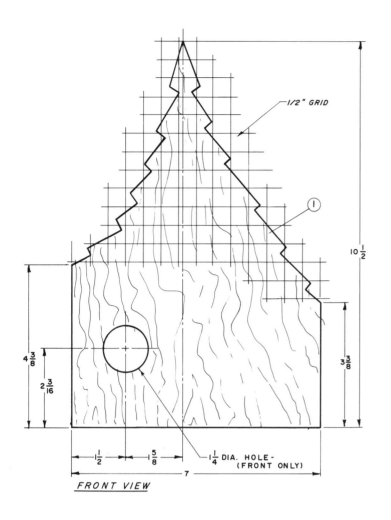

1/2" GRID

10 1/2

4 3/8

2 3/16

3 3/8

1 1/4 DIA. HOLE-
(FRONT ONLY)

1/2

5/8

7

FRONT VIEW

NO.	NAME	SIZE	REQ'D.
1	FRONT / BACK	1/2 X 7 - 10 1/2 LONG	2
2	SIDE - RIGHT	1/2 X 4 1/8 - 4 3/4	1
3	SIDE - LEFT	1/2 X 4 7/8 - 4 3/4	1
4	BOTTOM	1/2 X 4 3/4 - 6 LG.	1
5	PURCH	3/4 X 1 1/4 - 3 1/8 LG.	1
6	TRIM	1/4 X 1/4 - 6 1/2 LG.	1
7	TRIM	1/4 X 1/4 - 6 1/4 LG.	1
8	TRIM	1/4 X 1/4 - 4 LONG	1
9	TRIM	1/4 X 1/4 - 1 3/8 LG.	1
10	TRIM	1/4 X 1/4 - 4 3/8 LG.	1
11	TRIM	1/4 X 1/4 - 3 1/2 LG.	1
12	TRIM	1/4 X 1/4 - 3 3/4 LG.	1
13	TRIM	1/4 X 1/4 - 2 3/4 LG.	1
14	TRIM	1/4 X 1/4 - 3 1/2 LG.	1
15	ROOF	1/4 X 1 3/4 - 7 1/2	14

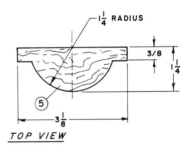

1 1/4 RADIUS

3/8

1 1/4

3 1/8

TOP VIEW

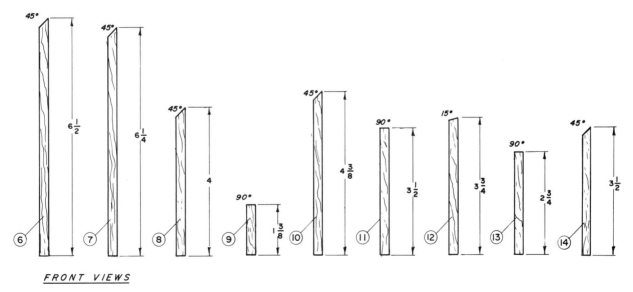

FRONT VIEWS

(Continued on following pages.)

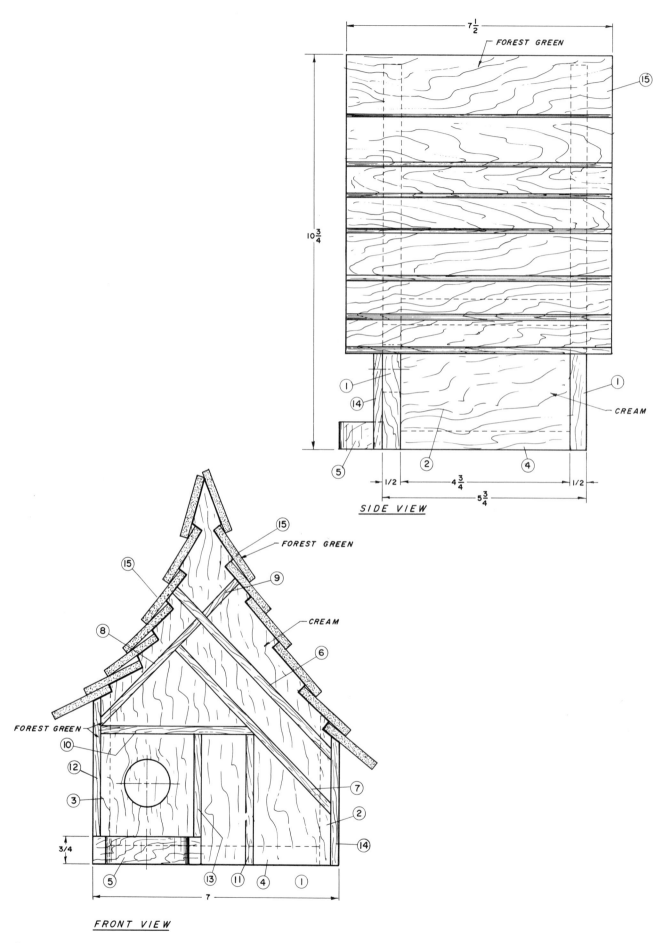

7½

FOREST GREEN

15

10¾

1
14
5

2

4

CREAM

1

1/2   4¾   1/2

5¾

SIDE VIEW

15

FOREST GREEN

15

9

CREAM

8

6

FOREST GREEN

10

7

12

2

3

14

3/4

5   13   11   4   1

7

FRONT VIEW

90

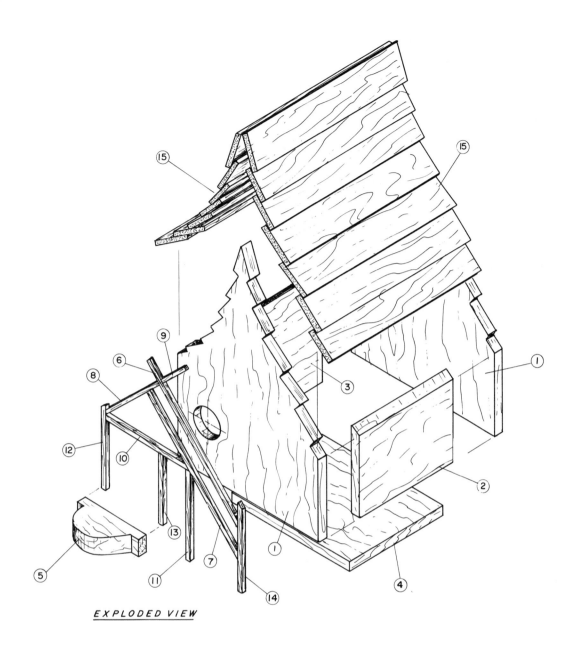

EXPLODED VIEW

♦**Step 4** Prime and paint using an exterior paint. Here comes the *fun* part; paint the trim boards as you wish. I painted mine forest green but you *could* match your house color. Now wait for spring; I'm sure you'll soon have it full of happy birds. (Especially if they appreciate "Victorian" architecture.)

30♦Cabinet with Heart

I never have enough storage space; I'm sure it's the same for you. Here is a small cupboard that is simple to make. Hearts seem to be everywhere just now, but they've been around for many years. Many Early American pieces incorporated a heart-shape cutout someplace in their design.

Instructions

♦Step 1   Cut all pieces to overall size.

♦Step 2   Using a 1-inch grid, lay out the top section of the backboard, part number 1, and top and bottom of the side, part number 2.

♦Step 3   Cut out the heart and profile. Sand all over.

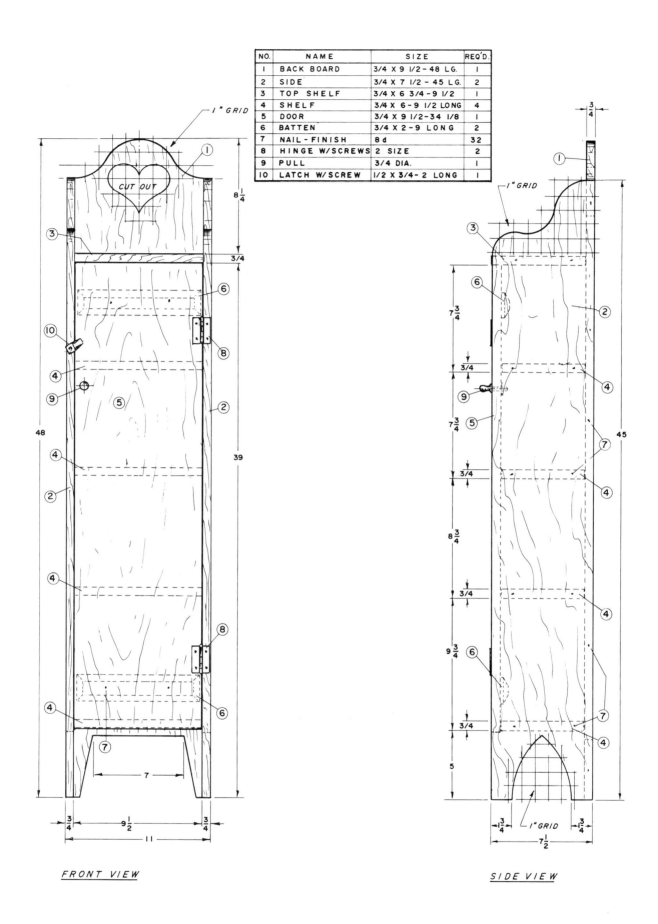

NO.	NAME	SIZE	REQ'D.
1	BACK BOARD	3/4 X 9 1/2 - 48 LG.	1
2	SIDE	3/4 X 7 1/2 - 45 LG.	2
3	TOP SHELF	3/4 X 6 3/4 - 9 1/2	1
4	SHELF	3/4 X 6 - 9 1/2 LONG	4
5	DOOR	3/4 X 9 1/2 - 34 1/8	1
6	BATTEN	3/4 X 2 - 9 LONG	2
7	NAIL - FINISH	8 d	32
8	HINGE W/SCREWS	2 SIZE	2
9	PULL	3/4 DIA.	1
10	LATCH W/SCREW	1/2 X 3/4 - 2 LONG	1

FRONT VIEW

SIDE VIEW

(Continued on next page.)

93

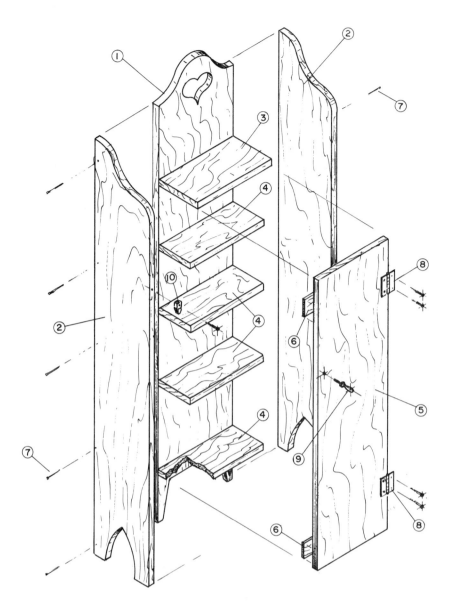

EXPLODED VIEW

◆**Step 4**   Assemble, keeping everything square as you go.

◆**Step 5**   Cut and fit the door using two hinges, parts number 8. Nail the batten straps, parts number 6, but do *not* glue; use nails only. Check that the door fits correctly.

◆**Step 6**   Locate and drill for the pull, part number 9.

◆**Step 7**   Remove the hinges, parts number 8. Prime and paint to suit.

◆**Step 8**   Reassemble the door, parts number 5 and 6. Add the latch, part number 10.

31 ♦ Folding Chair/Stool

I was reading a woodworking magazine a while ago and saw an appeal from a subscriber writing for plans for an antique chair that folded into a step stool. The subscriber sent a sketch of what he wanted. I had never seen such a chair/step stool, but thought it was a great idea.

From the sketch, I came up with my design of a chair/step stool. Since then, I have seen an ad for plans for a similar folding chair/stool, and recently I found an actual antique chair/step stool almost exactly like this one. I wish I had seen it before designing mine. It would have saved a lot of time.

(The instructions and the drawings are found on the following four pages.)

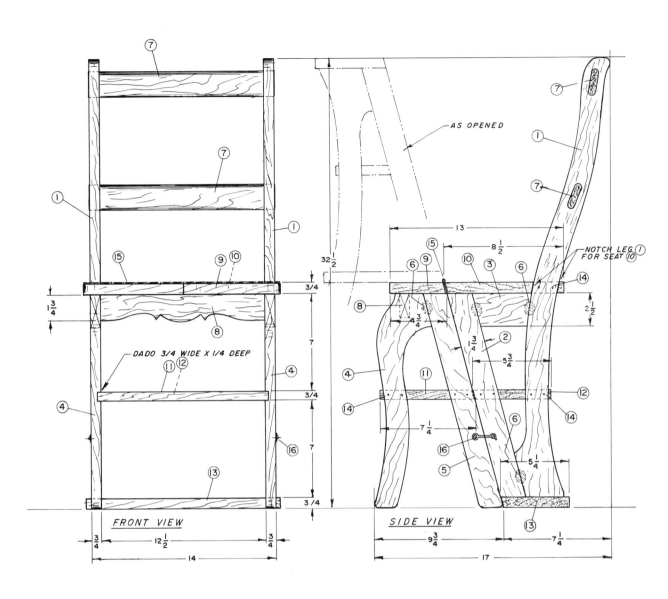

FRONT VIEW

DADO 3/4 WIDE X 1/4 DEEP

SIDE VIEW

AS OPENED

NOTCH LEG ① FOR SEAT ⑩

NO.	NAME	SIZE	REQ'D.
1	BACK LEG	3/4 X 4 - 32 1/2 LG.	2
2	BACK BRACE	3/4 X 1 3/4 - 15 3/4	2
3	RAIL	3/4 X 2 1/2 - 4 1/4	2
4	FRONT LEG	3/4 X 4 - 16 1/2 LG.	2
5	FRONT BRACE	3/4 X 1 3/4 - 16 5/8	2
6	BISQUIT	SIZE AS REQ'D.	8
7	BACK	3/4 X 2 1/4 X 14 LG	2
8	BRACE	3/4 X 1 3/4 - 12 1/2	1
9	SEAT FRONT	3/4 X 4 3/4 - 15 LG	1
10	SEAT BACK	3/4 X 8 1/2 -15 LG.	1
11	STEP	3/4 X 7 1/4 -13 LG.	1
12	STEP	3/4 X 5 3/4 -13 LG.	1
13	TOP STEP	3/4 X 5 1/4 -15 LG.	1
14	SCREW-FL. H D.	NO. 8-1 3/4 LONG	36
15	HINGE-PIANO	1" X 15 LONG	1
16	HOOK W/ SCREWS	LARGE	2

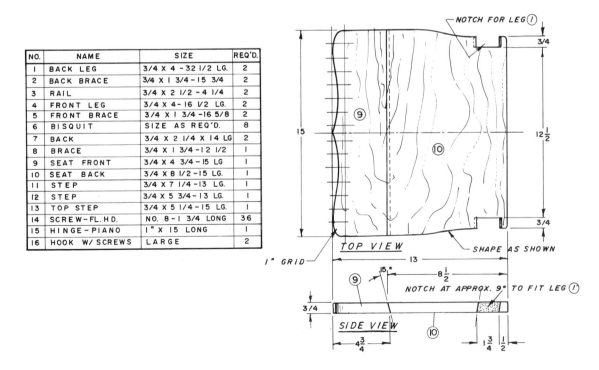

NOTCH FOR LEG ①

TOP VIEW

1" GRID

SHAPE AS SHOWN

NOTCH AT APPROX. 9° TO FIT LEG ①

SIDE VIEW

96

Instructions

♦**Step 1** Carefully study all of the plans to get an idea of how each part is made and how it all goes together.

♦**Step 2** Cut all parts to overall size. Use a hardwood such as ash or oak.

♦**Step 3** Lay out on a heavy piece of paper or cardboard the profiles of the back leg, front leg brace, and seat front, parts numbers 1 through 4, 8 and 9. Be sure to note the locations of all slots and dadoes.

♦**Step 4** Transfer your patterns to the wood and cut out. Be sure to make identical pairs.

♦**Step 5** Noting the detail plans, cut all of the other pieces to shape.
   Important: Do *not* cut any of the dadoes at this time; wait until after the sides are assembled.

♦**Step 6** Using a biscuit joiner, make all cuts in the ends of parts number 2,3,4,5, and 8, as shown in the drawings. You could dowel these parts if you do not have a biscuit joiner. (Continued on following pages.)

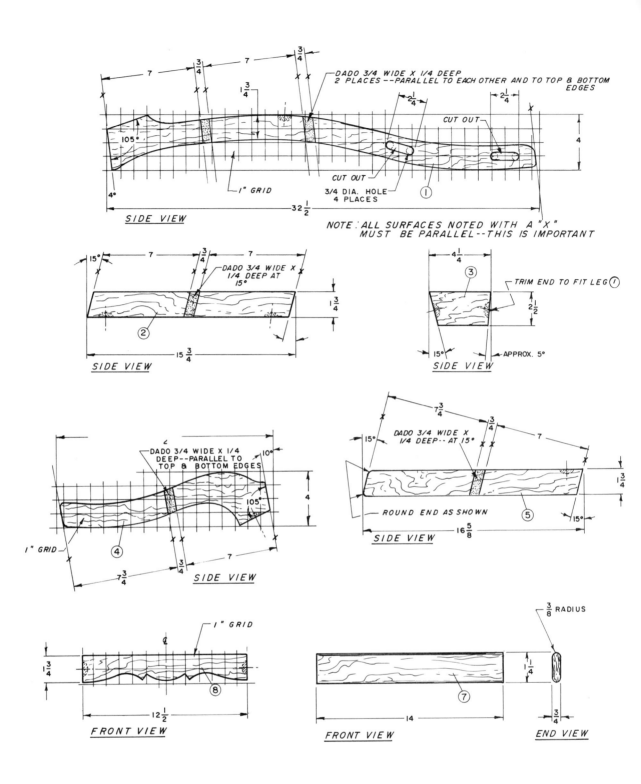

◆ Step 7 Assemble the sides using parts number 1 through 5. Make these subassemblies *exact* pairs.

◆ Step 8 Cut the ¾-inch-wide by ¼-inch-deep dadoes at this time as shown on *the inside* surfaces of parts number 1,2,4, and 5. Be sure to make a right-hand and left-hand pair of sides.

◆ Step 9 Complete the assembly. Take care that everything fits snugly. Since this will be stood on, be sure to glue all joints securely. Drill and nail the parts together if there is any doubt about strength.

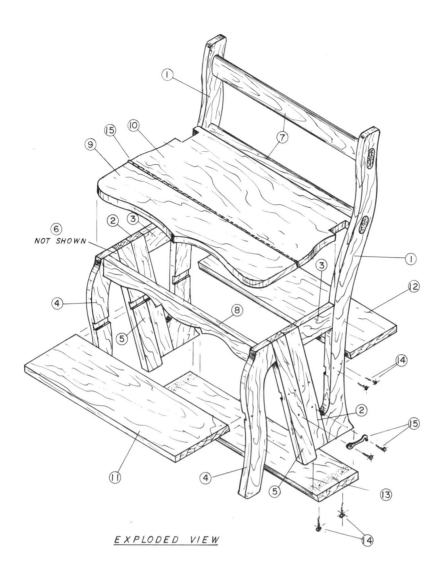

EXPLODED VIEW

♦**Step 10**   Add the piano hinge, part number 15, and check that the chair folds into a step stool—adjust as necessary.

♦**Step 11**   Remove the hinge and finish to suit. I used a clear gloss finish to show off the grain of the wood.

♦**Step 12**   Reattach the piano hinge, part number 15, and add the hook, part number 16. Check that it functions correctly.

32 ◆ Modern Bookcase

This modern bookcase is simple and functional. It is an ideal weekend project for beginning to intermediate woodworkers. You can adjust the lengths of the pieces to suit available wall lengths, if you wish.

Because it is so strong, solid red oak is a good wood to use. The unsupported span of shelf, nearly three feet, requires a sturdy wood to keep the shelf from sagging under a full load of books. You can use a weaker wood, provided that you shorten the length of the bookshelf so that the unsupported span is reduced. Clear white pine, for example, should not be used in shelf spans exceeding 24 inches.

Instructions

◆**Step 1**   Cut wood to size according to the materials list.

The back board, part 4, and kick board, part 5, are ripped to width after the sides, parts 1, and shelves, parts 2.

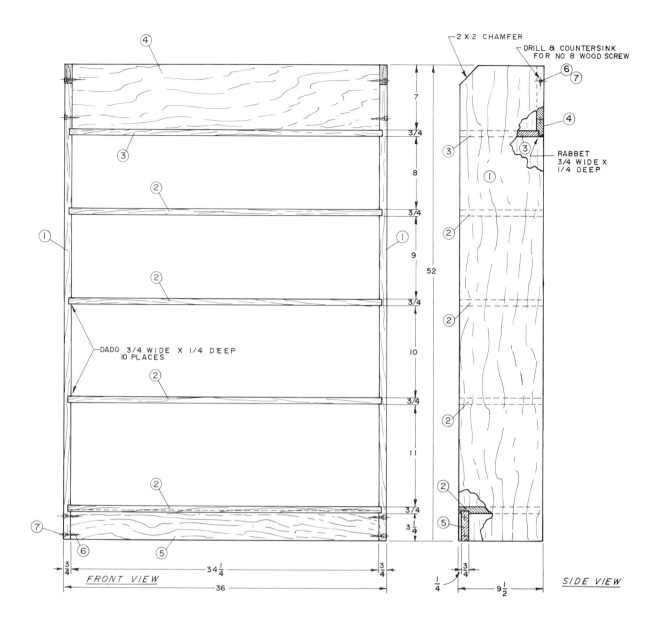

The radial-arm saw is the best tool for cutting the parts to length. Once the radial-arm saw is adjusted for square cuts, it may be easily set up for multiple operations. Set the saw up to square one end of each shelf, then slide the shelf to the other side of the table for the second cut. Use a stop block clamped to the radial-arm saw fence on the second cut, so that all of the shelves are exactly the same length. In three settings the cutting is done. The shelves, parts 2, are cut at 47 inches, the kick board and the back board at 46½ inches, and the sides, parts 1, at 42 inches. Check to be sure the corresponding parts are square and the same length.

♦ **Sept 2**   Lay out the dado locations in the end parts. A ¾-inch dado bit will leave a clean, flat-bottomed cut ready to be glued and assembled.

♦ **Step 3**   Cut the top front angle of each board.

♦ **Step 4**   Sand or plane all parts prior to assembly.

♦ **Step 5**   The shelves are now assembled with glue and screws. The screw holes are predrilled in the end boards first. The screws are countersunk to allow for plugs. (Continued on next page.)

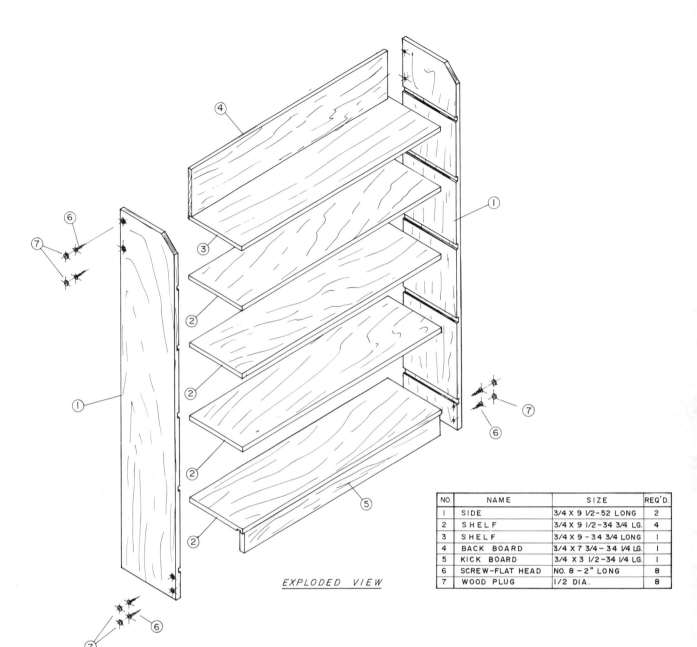

EXPLODED VIEW

NO.	NAME	SIZE	REQ'D.
1	SIDE	3/4 X 9 1/2-52 LONG	2
2	SHELF	3/4 X 9 1/2-34 3/4 LG.	4
3	SHELF	3/4 X 9 - 34 3/4 LONG	1
4	BACK BOARD	3/4 X 7 3/4 - 34 1/4 LG.	1
5	KICK BOARD	3/4 X 3 1/2-34 1/4 LG.	1
6	SCREW-FLAT HEAD	NO. 8 - 2" LONG	8
7	WOOD PLUG	1/2 DIA.	8

Note: Check the squareness of the case by measuring across the diagonals from opposite corners on the face of the bookcase.

◆**Step 6** Insert the top brace and kick board; screw in place. The kick board is designed not to touch the floor. The small gap left beneath the kick board will keep the bookcase resting square on the end boards in case there is a slight hump in the floor.

◆**Step 7** Cut plugs for the screw holes; glue in place with the grain of the plug following the grain in the end boards. Careful selection of plugs by color and grain will make the plug almost unnoticeable after sanding and finishing. Let the plugs stand proud of the finish surface while the glue dries. Later sand, file or shave the plugs to the finished surface. Then finish sanding.

◆**Step 8** The bookcase in the photograph was finished with four coats of "golden oak" oil finish; each applied one day apart. The third and fourth coats were whisk-sanded smooth with 360-grit sandpaper, and then a coat of wax was applied. To maintain the finish use a fine furniture polish.

33 ♦ Modern Plant Stand

While visiting a stylish craft shop along the seacoast of New Hampshire, I saw a fine display counter that I thought would make a great plant stand. Here is my version of that display counter.

Note: It is made entirely of ¾-inch by ¾-inch pieces.

Instructions

♦**Step 1** (The drawings are on the following two pages.) Cut all pieces to size. (Here is a chance to use up a lot of scrap wood.)

♦**Step 2** Make up eleven simple shelf assemblies using parts number 4 and 5. Be sure all eleven shelf assemblies are square and exactly the same size. Glue and nail together.

♦**Step 3** Locate and cut the ¾-inch-wide by ¼-inch-deep dadoes in parts number 1, 2 and 3. Use a jig or saw stop so that all 8 inch dimensions are exactly the same.

♦**Step 4** Drill a pilot hole in the center of each dado. Dado out a slot for the screws, parts number 6.

♦**Step 5** Now comes the *fun* part; putting it all together. (I would suggest you go out and get three or four friends to help.)

Working from left to right, assemble the plant stand following the drawing of the exploded view on the second page that follows. Glue and screw all joints; check as you proceed so that everything is square. (Continued on the following two pages.)

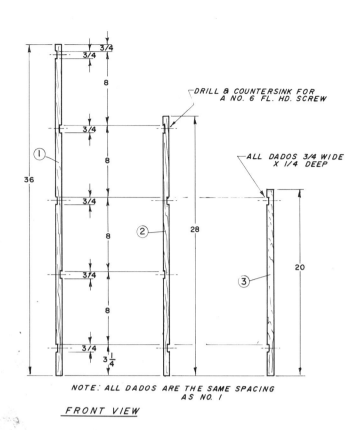

—DRILL & COUNTERSINK FOR
A NO. 6 FL. HD. SCREW

—ALL DADOS 3/4 WIDE
X 1/4 DEEP

NOTE: ALL DADOS ARE THE SAME SPACING
AS NO. I

FRONT VIEW

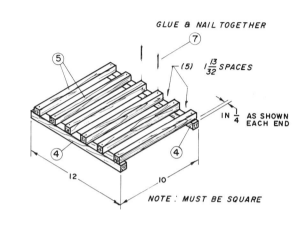

GLUE & NAIL TOGETHER

(5) $1\frac{13}{32}$ SPACES

IN $\frac{1}{4}$ AS SHOWN
EACH END

NOTE: MUST BE SQUARE

SUB-ASSEMBLY VIEW
(MAKE UP II UNITS AS SHOWN)

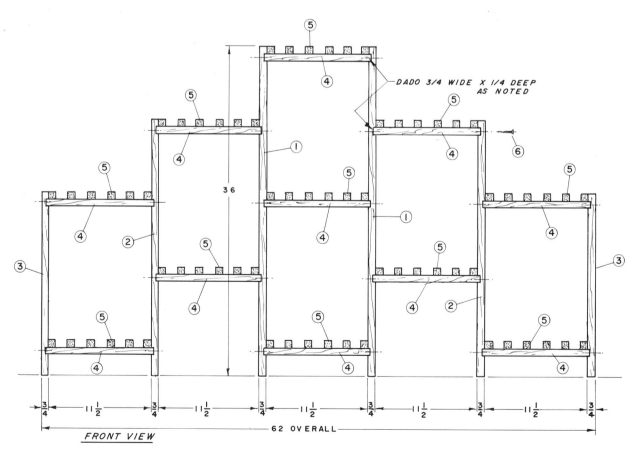

DADO 3/4 WIDE X 1/4 DEEP
AS NOTED

FRONT VIEW

62 OVERALL

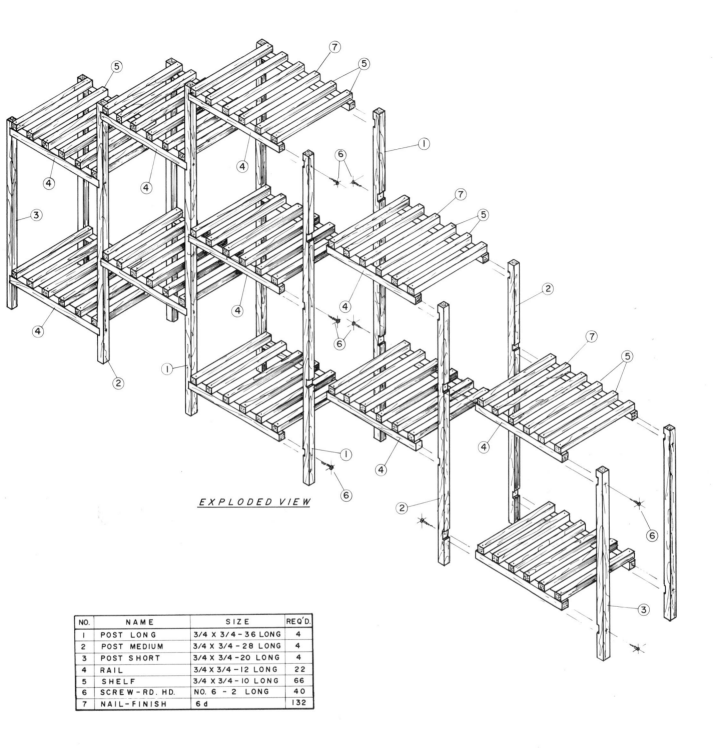

EXPLODED VIEW

NO.	NAME	SIZE	REQ'D.
1	POST LONG	3/4 X 3/4 – 36 LONG	4
2	POST MEDIUM	3/4 X 3/4 – 28 LONG	4
3	POST SHORT	3/4 X 3/4 – 20 LONG	4
4	RAIL	3/4 X 3/4 – 12 LONG	22
5	SHELF	3/4 X 3/4 – 10 LONG	66
6	SCREW – RD. HD.	NO. 6 – 2 LONG	40
7	NAIL – FINISH	6 d	132

◆**Step 6** Paint or stain to suit. If you have a paint sprayer, here is where
it will come in handy.

CLOCKS

34♦Jewelry Box Clock

This project is a takeoff of a small antique jewelry box I saw. The original was made of porcelain. This one is easy to make.

Instructions

♦**Step 1** Cut the center section out of a piece of hardwood that is 1$\frac{3}{8}$ inches thick, following the drawing.

♦**Step 2** Locate and drill a $\frac{3}{8}$-inch-diameter hole through as shown.

♦**Step 3** Glue a $\frac{1}{8}$-inch-thick piece to the bottom of the center section.

♦**Step 4** Drill a 2$\frac{5}{16}$-inch-diameter hole almost through the $\frac{1}{2}$-inch-thick lid. Do *not* drill all the way through.

♦**Step 5** Sand the bottom surface of the lid. From the *underside* of the lid, locate, and drill a $\frac{3}{8}$-inch-diameter hole, $\frac{3}{8}$ inch deep and also a $\frac{1}{8}$-inch-diameter hole, $\frac{1}{8}$ inch deep, as shown. Do not drill either hole through.

♦**Step 6** Cut a $\frac{3}{8}$-inch-diameter dowel 1$\frac{1}{2}$ inches long, and glue it into the hole in the lid.

♦**Step 7** Cut a $\frac{1}{8}$-inch-diameter dowel $\frac{1}{4}$ inch long, and glue it in place in the bottom surface of the lid. (This is a stop for the lid.)

♦**Step 8** Sand the top surface of the center section.

♦**Step 9** Attach the lid to the center and bottom section. Tack it in an out-of-the-way area, so that it cannot move or open.

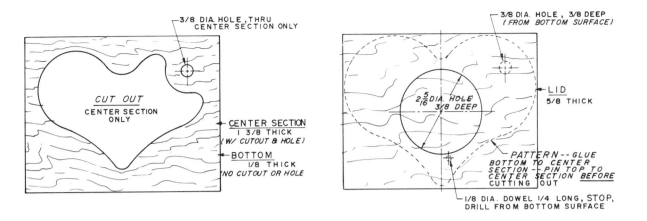

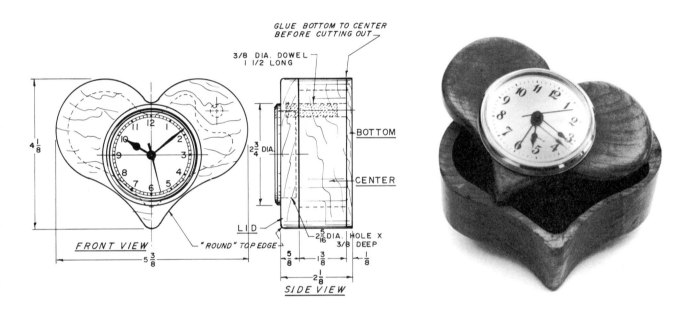

♦ **Step 10** Lay out the heart shape, and carefully cut it out. Sand the edges with the lid in place. Round the top edges as shown. Keep the bottom edge sharp. Check that the lid slides open correctly and that the stop works correctly.

♦ **Step 11** Remove the lid and apply a satin or gloss coat to suit.

♦ **Step 12** Add a battery to the clock; insert and place it into the lid. You might want to line the $2^5/_{16}$-inch-diameter opening.

Now you will have to go out and purchase some expensive jewelry!

35 ◆ "Joe Cool" Clock

Here is a clock for the young baseball fan. It should appeal to all kids.

Instructions

◆**Step 1**   Make a cardboard pattern of parts A,B,C, and D.

◆**Step 2**   Transfer the patterns to the wood, and carefully cut them out. Locate and drill the 2⁵⁄₁₆-inch-diameter hole before cutting out part A.

◆**Step 3**   Locate and glue part B to part A.

◆**Step 4**   Locate and glue part C to part B.

◆**Step 5**   Locate and drill part D to part B.

◆**Step 6**   Sand lightly all over, and round all edges slightly.

◆**Step 7**   Prime and paint "Joe" to suit.

◆**Step 8**   Add a battery to the clock; insert and attach it to the base. Your wall clock is ready to hang on the wall and be enjoyed for years to come.

PART 'A'

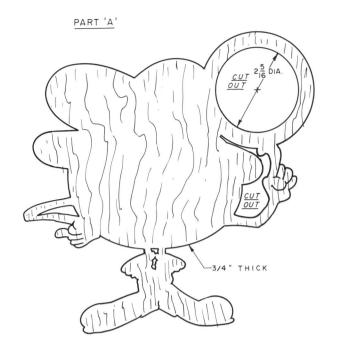

2 5/16 DIA.

CUT OUT

CUT OUT

3/4" THICK

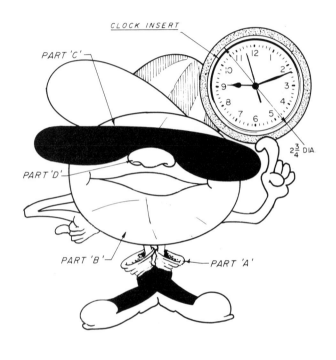

CLOCK INSERT

PART 'C'

PART 'D'

2 3/4 DIA.

PART 'B'

PART 'A'

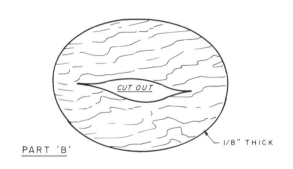

CUT OUT

PART 'B'

1/8" THICK

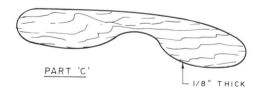

PART 'C'

1/8" THICK

PART 'D'

1/4" THICK

36 ♦ Triangle Clock

This is a modern shelf clock that can be left clear or that can be painted. It is easy to make and is a great seller at a craft fair.

Instructions

♦**Step 1**   Cut the body, part number 1, to size. If you do not have 1¾-inch thick material, simply glue up ½-inch or ¾-inch thick material.

♦**Step 2**   Locate and drill a 3⅜-inch-diameter hole.

♦**Step 3**   Cut to shape, and sand all surfaces with fine sandpaper.

♦**Step 4**   Using a ³⁄₃₂-inch-radius cove cutter with a ball-bearing follower, cut a radius around the outer edge as shown.

♦**Step 5**   Drill a hole for the center shaft of the movement.

♦**Step 6**   Finish to suit. Add feet, parts number 4.

♦**Step 7**   Add a battery to the clock movement, and add to the body.

♦**Step 8**   Add hands—and set the correct time!

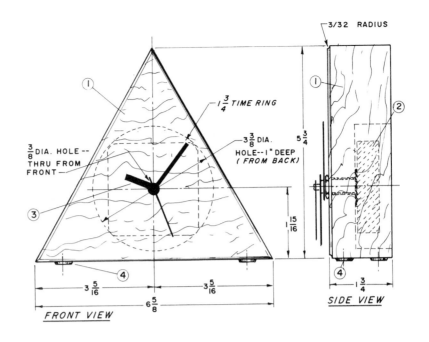

3/32 RADIUS

1 3/4 TIME RING

3/8 DIA. HOLE--
THRU FROM
FRONT

3 3/8 DIA.
HOLE--1" DEEP
(FROM BACK)

5 3/4

1 15/16

3 5/16

3 5/16

6 5/8

1 3/4

FRONT VIEW

SIDE VIEW

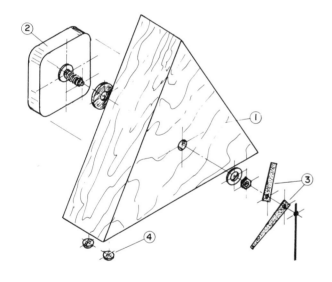

EXPLODED VIEW

NO.	NAME	SIZE	REQ'D.
1	BODY	1 3/4 X 5 3/4-6 5/8	1
2	QUARTZ MOVEMENT	LONG STEM	1
3	HANDS (1 1/2 SIZE)	MODERN STYLE	1 PR.
4	FOOT	1/2 SIZE	4

37◆Notepad Clock

This clock is a handy clock. Placed next to a telephone it is great, since you can keep notepaper in it for taking telephone messages.

Instructions

◆**Step 1**   Cut all of the pieces to overall size. Sand all surfaces, keeping all of the edges sharp.

◆**Step 2**   Locate and drill the 2⅛-inch-diameter hole for the insert. Cut the two 45 degree top edges.

◆**Step 3**   Assemble the back board, front, and sides together—parts number 1,2, and 3.

◆**Step 4**   Cut a ¼-inch-wide by ¼-inch-deep dado *around* the bottom inside surface as shown at view A–A.

◆**Step 5**   Cut the bottom, part number 4, to size, and tack it in place. Do *not* glue. Make a loose fit to allow for expansion.

◆**Step 6**   Finish to suit.

◆**Step 7**   Add a battery to the clock movement, and insert it into the hole.

◆**Step 8**   Add the feet and paper, parts number 7 and 8. It's all set for years of use.

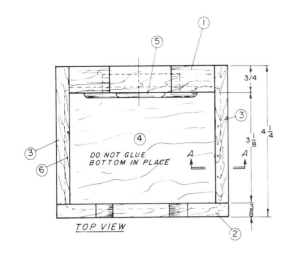

3/4

4 1/4

3 1/8

3/8

① ⑤ ①

④ DO NOT GLUE BOTTOM IN PLACE

③ ③

⑥

A A

②

TOP VIEW

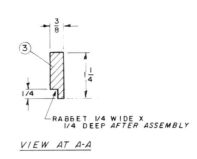

3/8

③

1 1/4

1/4

RABBET 1/4 WIDE X 1/4 DEEP AFTER ASSEMBLY

VIEW AT A-A

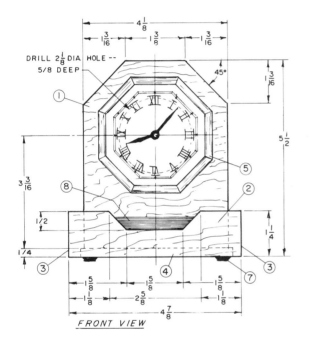

4 1/8

1 3/16   1 3/8   1 3/16

DRILL 2 1/8 DIA HOLE -- 5/8 DEEP

45°

1 3/16

5 1/2

①

⑤

②

3 3/16

⑧

1/2

1/4

1 1/4

③ ④ ⑦ ③

5/8   5/8   5/8

1 1/8   2 5/8   1 1/8

4 7/8

FRONT VIEW

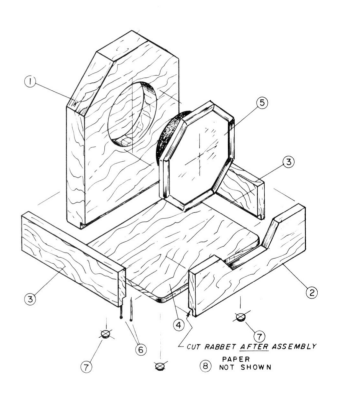

①

⑤

③

③

④

⑥

⑦

②

CUT RABBET AFTER ASSEMBLY

⑦

PAPER NOT SHOWN ⑧

EXPLODED VIEW

NO.	NAME	SIZE	REQ'D.
1	BACK BOARD	3/4 X 5 1/2 - 4 1/8 LG.	1
2	FRONT	3/8 X 1 1/4 - 4 7/8 LG.	1
3	SIDE	3/8 X 1 1/4 - 3 7/8 LG.	2
4	BOTTOM	1/4 X 3 5/8 - 4 5/8	1
5	CLOCK - OCTAGON		1
6	BRAD	3/4 LONG	4
7	FOOT OR PAD	1/2 DIA.	4
8	PAPER	3 X 4 SIZE	1

38 ◆ Modern Shelf Clock

This unusual clock has no hands. In their place are thin round discs with a ⁵⁄₁₆-inch-diameter walnut dot to point out the hour and minute. If nothing else, it is different.

Instructions

◆**Step 1**   Study the plans carefully.
   Note: There are three cutting steps in the body, part number 1. Be sure to cut them in the order suggested.

◆**Step 2**   Cut all of the pieces to overall size; then lightly sand all over. If you want to add the optional stripes in part number 2, glue up material to suit and sand to ¼ inch thick.

◆**Step 3**   Cut the overall shape of the body, part number 1. Sand all over. Using a ¼-inch-wide router bit with a ball-bearing follower, make the ¼-inch-wide dado (*first cut*) on the *inside* surface ⅜ of an inch in from the front edge.

◆**Step 4**   Using a ⅛-inch-radius router bit with a ball-bearing follower make the *second cut* around the inside, front edge. Using the same bit, make the *third cut* around the outside, front edge.

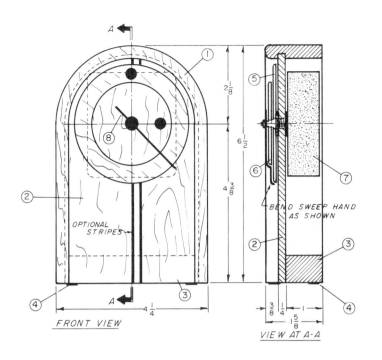

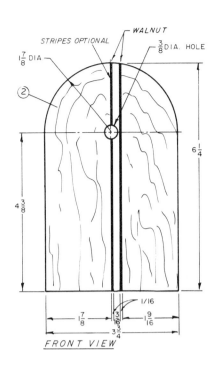

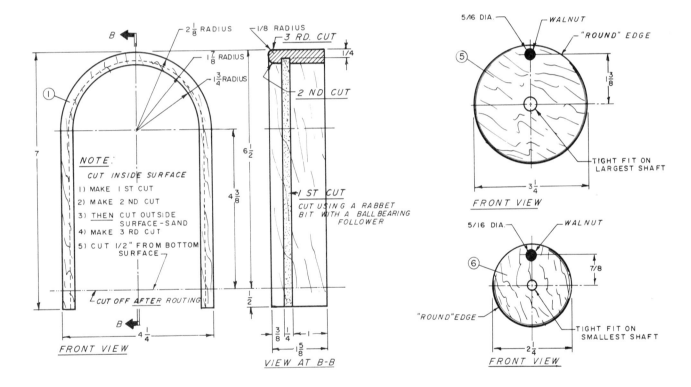

♦**Step 5** Cut to length *after* routing steps 1,2, and 3.

♦**Step 6** Cut and fit the face, part number 2, into the ¼-inch-wide slot in the body, part number 1. Glue in place.

♦**Step 7** Add the bottom, part number 3, in place.

♦**Step 8** Sand all over and finish to suit. (Continued on next page.)

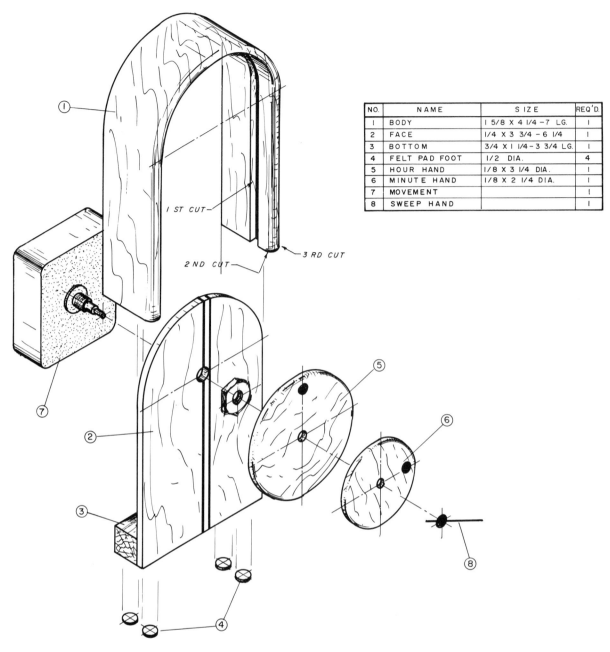

NO.	NAME	SIZE	REQ'D.
1	BODY	1 5/8 X 4 1/4 – 7 LG.	1
2	FACE	1/4 X 3 3/4 – 6 1/4	1
3	BOTTOM	3/4 X 1 1/4 – 3 3/4 LG.	1
4	FELT PAD FOOT	1/2 DIA.	4
5	HOUR HAND	1/8 X 3 1/4 DIA.	1
6	MINUTE HAND	1/8 X 2 1/4 DIA.	1
7	MOVEMENT		1
8	SWEEP HAND		1

EXPLODED VIEW

◆ **Step 9** Add the movement.

◆ **Step 10** Fit the hour disc, part number 5. It should have a tight fit, so that it will not slip.

◆ **Step 11** Fit the minute disc, part number 6. It, too, should fit tightly and not slip.

39 ◆ Tambour Clock

My book, 52 *Weekend Woodworking Projects* (STERLING, 1991), has a full-size tambour clock in it. It is an exact copy of an antique tambour clock (circa 1910). I usually find tambour clocks quite ugly, but this particular one has very nice lines. I liked it so much, I took the original design and reduced it in size. I think that made at this size, it especially makes a very attractive clock.

Instructions

◆**Step 1** (The drawings are on the following page.) If you don't have a piece of wood four inches thick you will have to glue up material to get the thickness.

◆**Step 2** Lay out and transfer the shape of the body, part number 1, to the wood. Carefully cut and sand all surfaces. Keep all of the edges sharp.

◆**Step 3** Cut and route the ⅛-inch radius in the base.

◆**Step 4** Lay out and cut the small moulding piece, part number 3. I laid out the *inner* edge only and cut it out. I then cut the ⅛-inch-radius cove cut. *After* the inside cuts are made, I made the *outer* edge cut. By doing it this way, you have something to hold on to while making the ⅛-inch-radius cove cut.

◆**Step 5** Locate and drill the hole for the insert.

◆**Step 6** Glue the moulding, part number 3, to the body, part number 1. Sand the edge.

◆**Step 7** Add the base, part number 2.

◆**Step 8** Sand and finish to suit. (Continued on next page.)

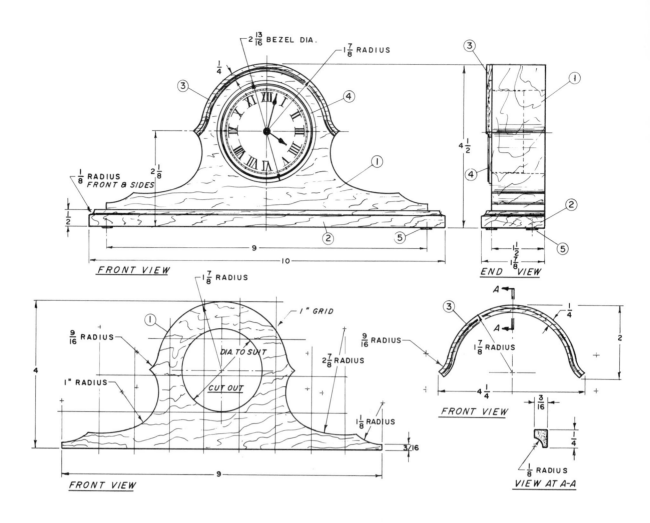

FRONT VIEW

END VIEW

FRONT VIEW

FRONT VIEW

VIEW AT A-A

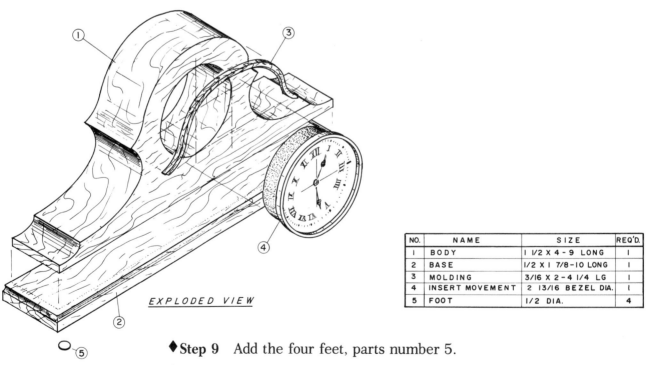

EXPLODED VIEW

NO.	NAME	SIZE	REQ'D.
1	BODY	1 1/2 X 4 - 9 LONG	1
2	BASE	1/2 X 1 7/8 - 10 LONG	1
3	MOLDING	3/16 X 2 - 4 1/4 LG	1
4	INSERT MOVEMENT	2 13/16 BEZEL DIA.	1
5	FOOT	1/2 DIA.	4

◆**Step 9** Add the four feet, parts number 5.

◆**Step 10** Fit and insert the movement, and set the correct time. Your "new" antique is ready to be used for years to come.

118

40 ◆ Modern Wall Clock

If your home decor is contemporary, this wall clock is for you. It is easy to make and can be finished many ways to blend into any room color.

Instructions

◆ **Step 1** (The drawings are on the following pages.) Cut all pieces to overall size. Sand all surfaces.

◆ **Step 2** Cut the radius at the ends of the base, part number 1, and sand. Using a ⅛-inch-radius cove cutter, with a ball-bearing follower cut the outer edge as shown.

◆ **Step 3** Lay out and cut to size a doughnut-shaped piece for the outer ring, part number 2. Cove-cut the front, outer edge like the base. Using a router bit with a ball-bearing follower cut the inside rabbet ¼-inch wide and ⅜-inch deep for the inner ring, part number 3. (Continued on next page.)

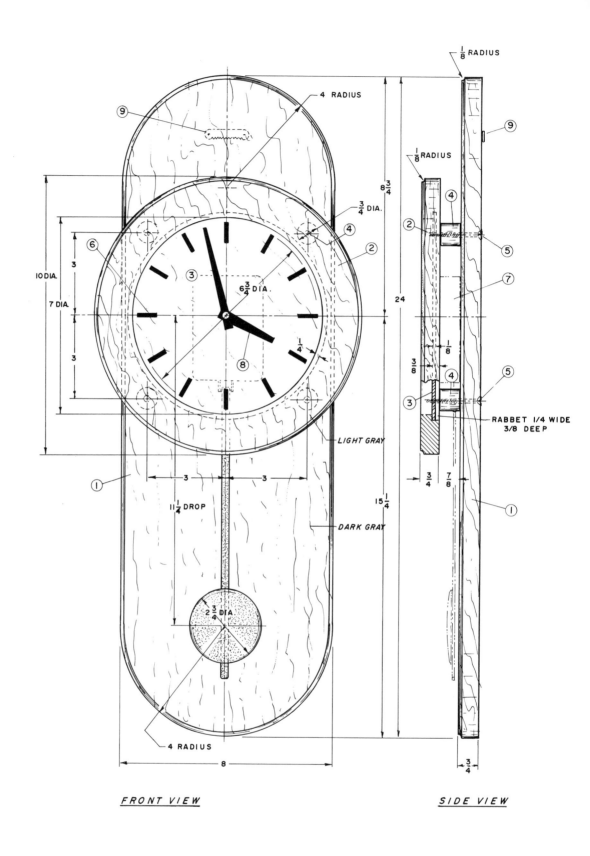

FRONT VIEW   SIDE VIEW

♦**Step 4**   Cut the inner ring, part number 3, to size, and fit it to the outer ring, part number 2. Drill the center hole for the center shaft.

♦**Step 5**   Glue the inner ring, part number 3, into the outer ring, part number 2. Be sure that the direction of the grain is the same in both pieces.

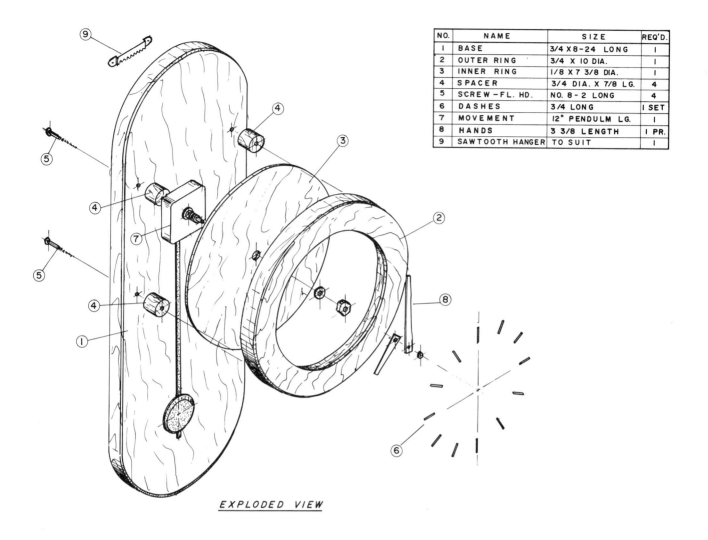

NO.	NAME	SIZE	REQ'D.
1	BASE	3/4 X 8-24 LONG	1
2	OUTER RING	3/4 X 10 DIA.	1
3	INNER RING	1/8 X 7 3/8 DIA.	1
4	SPACER	3/4 DIA. X 7/8 LG.	4
5	SCREW-FL. HD.	NO. 8-2 LONG	4
6	DASHES	3/4 LONG	1 SET
7	MOVEMENT	12" PENDULM LG.	1
8	HANDS	3 3/8 LENGTH	1 PR.
9	SAWTOOTH HANGER	TO SUIT	1

EXPLODED VIEW

♦**Step 6**   Cut the spacers, parts number 4, to length from a ¾-inch-diameter dowel. Drill a ⅛-inch-diameter hole through the center of each.

♦**Step 7**   Locate and drill four ⅛-inch-diameter holes for the screws, parts number 5, in the base, part number 1. Countersink the holes *from the back* for the four screws, parts number 5.

♦**Step 8**   Carefully locate and drill 4¹⁄₁₆-inch-diameter holes in the *back* surface of the outer ring, part number 2. They should line up *exactly* as the four holes in the base, part number 1. Temporarily assemble the pieces to check for fit. Disassemble.

♦**Step 9**   Sand all over and finish all of the pieces to suit.
   Note: This project could be made of a wood such as ash or oak and finished in a clear coat to show the grain, or painted with a color that accents the room it will be placed in.

♦**Step 10**   Glue the twelve dashes in place. (Use a 6¾-inch time ring.) Add the hanger, part number 9.

♦**Step 11**   Assemble all of the pieces following the drawing of the exploded view above. Add a battery, pendulum, and the hands. The clock is ready for hanging.

41◆Dog Wall Clock

This project is a dog! (Bad pun, I know.) This is *my* kind of dog. You don't have to feed it, clean up after it, walk it, or listen to it bark. This is a real *fun* project and will be enjoyed by children for many years to come. It requires a special movement with a pendulum at the top *and* bottom.

Instructions

◆**Step 1** *Carefully* study how it all goes together and how all pieces are made.

   Important: Keep the tail and ears as *light* as possible so it will work correctly.

◆**Step 2** Cut all pieces of wood to overall size and sand. Be sure to use good-quality plywood for the thin pieces.

◆**Step 3** Carefully lay out the pattern for each piece and transfer each to the wood. Cut all irregular pieces to shape.

◆**Step 4** Locate and drill all holes in the pieces. Sand lightly.

◆**Step 5** Temporarily fit the block, part number 9, to the pendulum at the *top* of the movement. Glue the ears, parts number 8, to the block, part number 9. Add enough washers (two or three), parts number 10, to balance the weight of the ears.

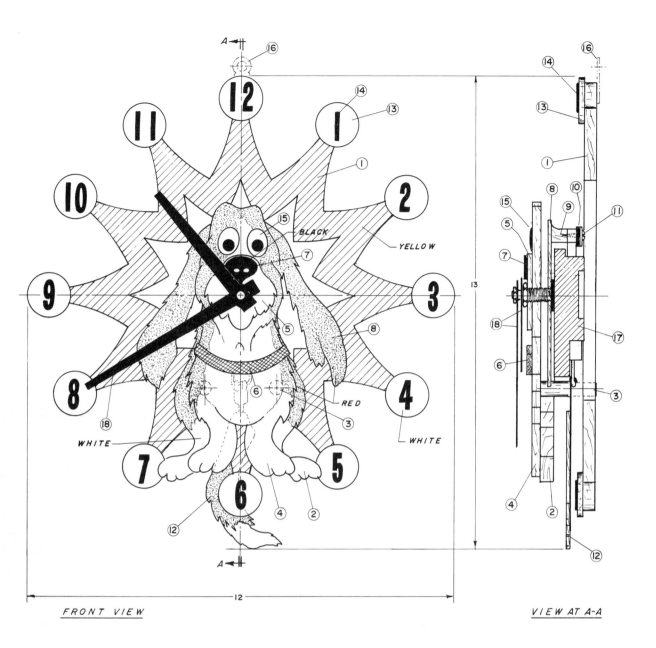

FRONT VIEW

VIEW AT A-A

◆**Step 6**   Epoxy the lower pendulum to the tail, part number 12.

◆**Step 7**   Glue the back body, part number 2, to the front body, part number 4. Take care to line up the hole for the center shaft.

◆**Step 8**   Glue the cheeks, parts number 5, to the body, part number 4. Glue the nose, part number 7, to the cheeks, parts number 5, and add the collar, part number 6.

◆**Step 9**   Cut a 1¼-inch-diameter dowel into ⅛-inch-thick slivers and sand. These will be the twelve supports, parts number 13.

◆**Step 10**   Glue the twelve supports, parts number 13, to the base, part number 1. Add the hanger, part number 16.

◆**Step 11**   Here is the *fun* part. Paint your clock to suit. You can have a bright dog or whatever color combination you wish. (Continued on the following two pages.)

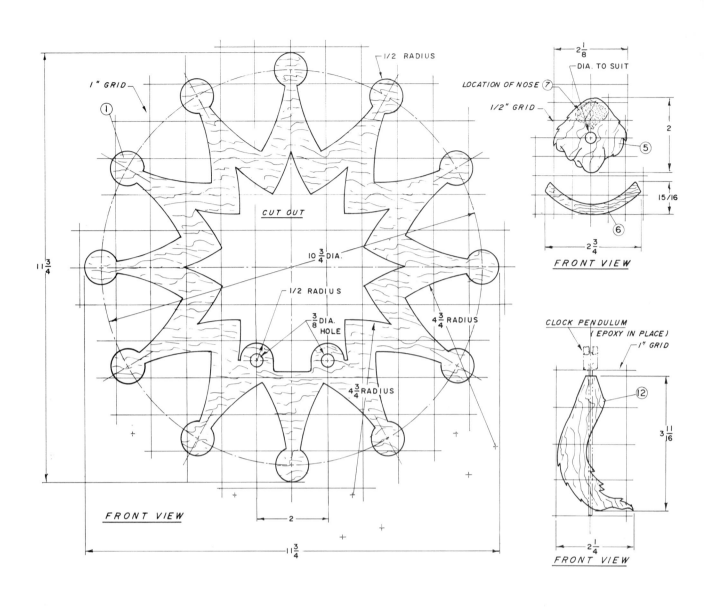

1" GRID

1/2 RADIUS

①

CUT OUT

10 3/4 DIA.

1/2 RADIUS

3/8 DIA. HOLE

4 3/4 RADIUS

4 3/4 RADIUS

11 3/4

FRONT VIEW

2

11 3/4

2 1/8

DIA. TO SUIT

LOCATION OF NOSE ⑦

1/2" GRID

⑤

2

15/16

⑥

2 3/4

FRONT VIEW

CLOCK PENDULUM
(EPOXY IN PLACE)

1" GRID

⑫

3 11/16

2 1/4

FRONT VIEW

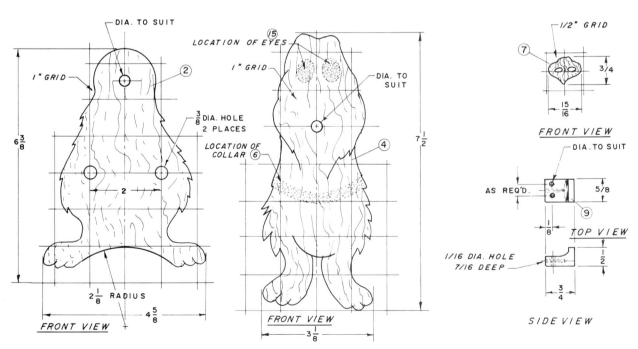

DIA. TO SUIT

1" GRID

②

3/8 DIA. HOLE
2 PLACES

6 3/8

2

2 1/8 RADIUS

4 5/8

FRONT VIEW

⑮ LOCATION OF EYES

1" GRID

DIA. TO SUIT

LOCATION OF COLLAR ⑥

④

7 1/2

FRONT VIEW

3 3/8

1/2" GRID

⑦

3/4

15/16

FRONT VIEW

DIA. TO SUIT

AS REQ'D.

5/8

⑨

1/8

TOP VIEW

1/16 DIA. HOLE
7/16 DEEP

1/2

3/4

SIDE VIEW

124

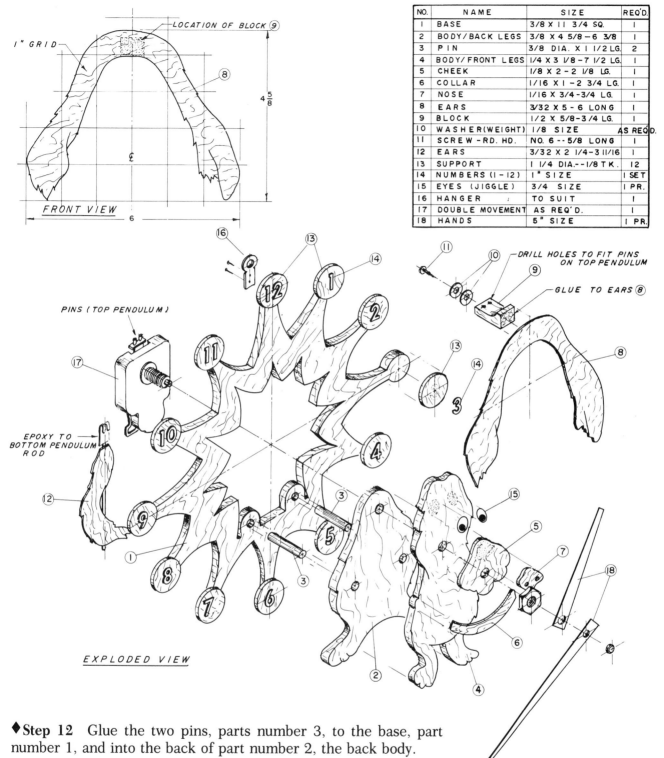

LOCATION OF BLOCK ⑨

1" GRID

FRONT VIEW

$4\frac{5}{8}$

6

NO.	NAME	SIZE	REQ'D.
1	BASE	3/8 X 11 3/4 SQ.	1
2	BODY/BACK LEGS	3/8 X 4 5/8 – 6 3/8	1
3	PIN	3/8 DIA. X 1 1/2 LG.	2
4	BODY/FRONT LEGS	1/4 X 3 1/8 – 7 1/2 LG.	1
5	CHEEK	1/8 X 2 – 2 1/8 LG.	1
6	COLLAR	1/16 X 1 – 2 3/4 LG.	1
7	NOSE	1/16 X 3/4 – 3/4 LG.	1
8	EARS	3/32 X 5 – 6 LONG	1
9	BLOCK	1/2 X 5/8 – 3/4 LG.	1
10	WASHER (WEIGHT)	1/8 SIZE	AS REQ'D.
11	SCREW – RD. HD.	NO. 6 – – 5/8 LONG	1
12	EARS	3/32 X 2 1/4 – 3 11/16	1
13	SUPPORT	1 1/4 DIA. – –1/8 T K.	12
14	NUMBERS (1 – 12)	1" SIZE	1 SET
15	EYES (JIGGLE)	3/4 SIZE	1 PR.
16	HANGER	TO SUIT	1
17	DOUBLE MOVEMENT	AS REQ'D.	1
18	HANDS	5" SIZE	1 PR.

PINS (TOP PENDULUM)

DRILL HOLES TO FIT PINS ON TOP PENDULUM

GLUE TO EARS ⑧

EPOXY TO BOTTOM PENDULUM ROD

EXPLODED VIEW

◆**Step 12** Glue the two pins, parts number 3, to the base, part number 1, and into the back of part number 2, the back body.

◆**Step 13** Epoxy the block, part number 9, *with* the ears and weights attached to the top pendulum base.

◆**Step 14** Attach the movement to the body assembly, and bolt it in place.

◆**Step 15** Add the hands and lower pendulum assembly.

◆**Step 16** Glue the twelve numbers, parts number 14, in place. Glue the eyes, parts number 15 in place.

◆**Step 17** If everything is okay attach to a wall and give the tail a push.

COUNTRY PROJECTS

42 ◆ Country Mirror

This is a takeoff of a larger country mirror I saw in a museum years ago. The original was about one-third larger. Scaled down it makes a suitable mirror for use in a child's room or in a small room. It will add a "country" look wherever it is hung. The original was painted a mustard color, but it looks good either painted or stained.

Instructions

◆ **Step 1**   Cut the body to overall size.

◆ **Step 2**   Carefully lay out the outer and interior details of the body, part number 1. Transfer the shape to the wood and cut out. Drill a ½-inch hole at the top, as shown in the drawings.

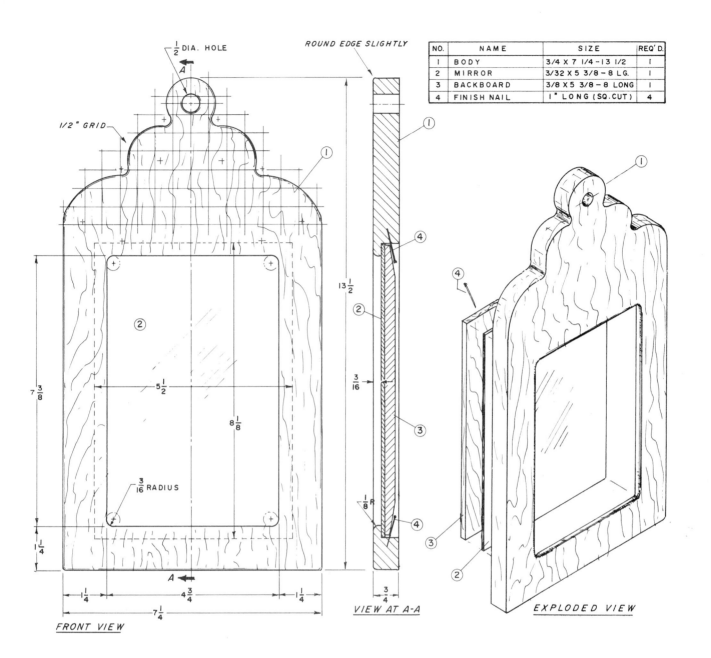

NO.	NAME	SIZE	REQ'D.
1	BODY	3/4 X 7 1/4 - 13 1/2	1
2	MIRROR	3/32 X 5 3/8 - 8 LG.	1
3	BACKBOARD	3/8 X 5 3/8 - 8 LONG	1
4	FINISH NAIL	1" LONG (SQ. CUT)	4

FRONT VIEW

VIEW AT A-A

EXPLODED VIEW

◆**Step 3**   Using a straight router bit with a ball-bearing follower, make a rabbet cut on the inside cutout, back surface for the mirror, part number 2.

◆**Step 4**   Using a ⅛-inch-radius router bit with a ball-bearing follower, round the front edges inside and out, as shown.

◆**Step 5**   Cut the back board, part number 3, to size (to fit the opening). Cut the back edge on a sharp bevel (10 degrees or so) as shown in the view A–A.

◆**Step 6**   Sand all over.

◆**Step 7**   Paint or stain to suit. (If you paint this, distress it slightly to look somewhat old.)

◆**Step 8**   Add the mirror, part number 1, and back board, part number 3, with the nails, parts number 4.

43 ♦ Wall Box with Heart

Wall boxes are always popular. They come in all shapes and sizes. This is a fancy wall box. It is *not* an exact copy of an antique; it is simply a composite of two or three antique wall boxes that I have liked.

Instructions

♦ **Step 1** Cut material to overall size. Sand all over.

♦ **Step 2** Lay out the patterns for the pieces. Transfer the shapes to the wood, and cut them out.

♦ **Step 3** Dry-fit all of the pieces. If everything fits correctly, nail the pieces together. Keep everything sharp and square as you go.

♦ **Step 4** Prime; then paint or stain to suit.

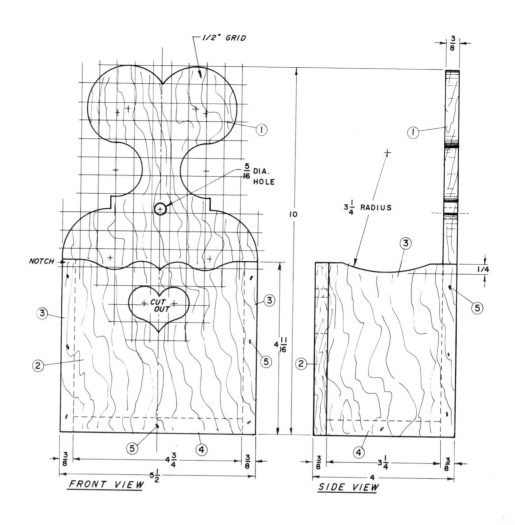

1/2" GRID

5/16 DIA. HOLE

3/8

3 1/4 RADIUS

10

NOTCH

CUT OUT

4 11/16

1/4

3/8   4 3/4   3/8
5 1/2

3/8   3 1/4   3/8
4

FRONT VIEW

SIDE VIEW

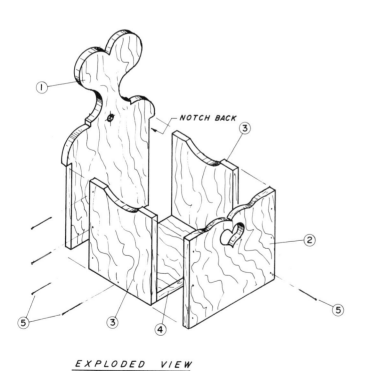

NOTCH BACK

EXPLODED VIEW

NO.	NAME	SIZE	REQ'D.
I	BACK	3/8 X 5 1/2 - 10 LG.	I
2	FRONT	3/8 X 5 1/2 - 4 11/16	I
3	SIDE	3/8 X 3 5/8 - 4 11/16	2
4	BOTTOM	3/8 X 3 1/4 - 4 3/4	I
5	SQ. CUT NAIL FINISH	1" LONG	15

44 ◆ Salt Box

This is a scaled-down version of a somewhat larger salt box. The original was painted a dark blackish green color.

Instructions

◆**Step 1** Cut material to overall size. Sand all over.

◆**Step 2** Lay out the patterns for the pieces. Transfer the shapes to the wood, and cut them out.

◆**Step 3** Dry-fit all of the pieces. If everything fits correctly, nail the pieces together. Keep everything sharp and square as you go.

◆**Step 4** Prime; then paint or stain to suit.

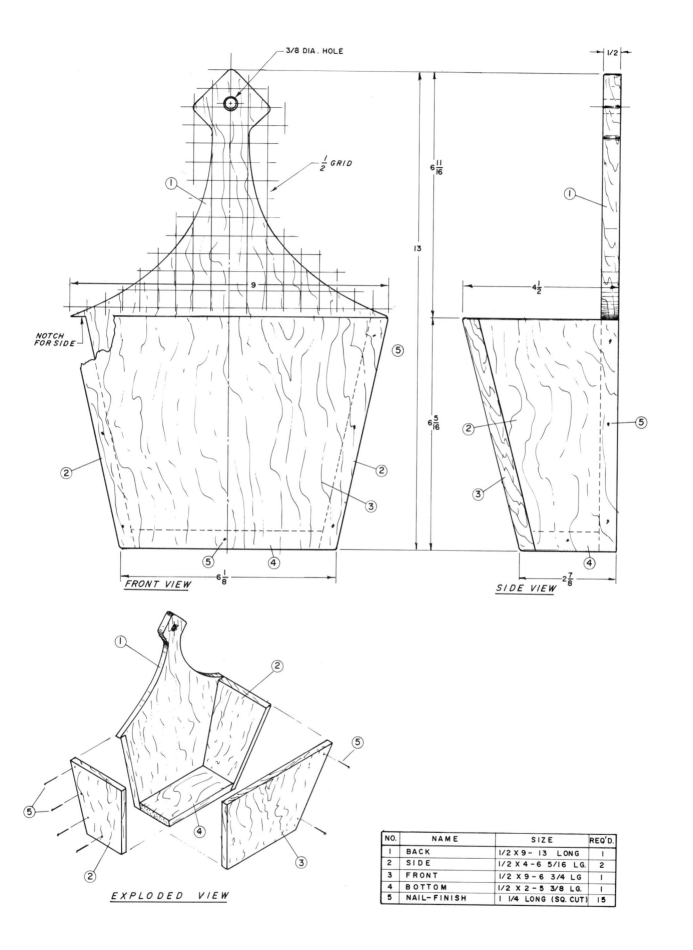

3/8 DIA. HOLE

$\frac{1}{2}$ GRID

1/2

$6\frac{11}{16}$

13

$6\frac{5}{16}$

9

NOTCH
FOR SIDE

$4\frac{1}{2}$

FRONT VIEW

$6\frac{1}{8}$

SIDE VIEW

$2\frac{7}{8}$

EXPLODED VIEW

NO.	NAME	SIZE	REQ'D.
1	BACK	1/2 X 9 - 13 LONG	1
2	SIDE	1/2 X 4 - 6 5/16 LG.	2
3	FRONT	1/2 X 9 - 6 3/4 LG	1
4	BOTTOM	1/2 X 2 - 5 3/8 LG.	1
5	NAIL-FINISH	1 1/4 LONG (SQ. CUT)	15

45 ♦ Cranberry Scoop

This is a copy of a real cranberry scoop that was used in the cranberry bogs of Massachusetts. Today, this scoop makes a functional wall decoration for plants or, perhaps, out-going mail. Or you could use it for a small magazine rack. If you use old wood—or if you distress new wood—yours will look like the original.

Instructions

♦**Step 1** Cut all of the pieces to overall size.
  Note: One of each of parts numbers 2, 3, and 4 will be cut one inch shorter (to a 7-inch length).

♦**Step 2** The shape of the handle, part number 7, will have to be laid out on a 1-inch grid and cut out.

♦**Step 3** Cut an inch off one of the two, parts numbers 2, 3 and 4. The 8-inch-long piece is for the *front*; the 7-inch-long one is for the *back*.

♦**Step 4** Locate and drill nine ⅜-inch-diameter holes along the *top* edge of the 7-inch-long back board, part number 2. Use the given dimensions at the top of the front view.

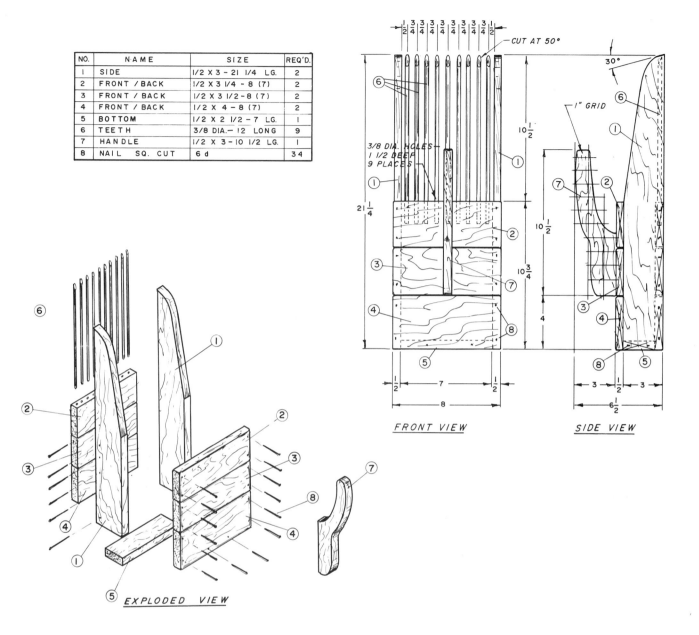

NO.	NAME	SIZE	REQ'D.
I	SIDE	1/2 X 3 - 21 1/4 LG.	2
2	FRONT / BACK	1/2 X 3 1/4 - 8 (7)	2
3	FRONT / BACK	1/2 X 3 1/2 - 8 (7)	2
4	FRONT / BACK	1/2 X 4 - 8 (7)	2
5	BOTTOM	1/2 X 2 1/2 - 7 LG.	I
6	TEETH	3/8 DIA.- 12 LONG	9
7	HANDLE	1/2 X 3 -10 1/2 LG.	I
8	NAIL SQ. CUT	6 d	34

FRONT VIEW

SIDE VIEW

EXPLODED VIEW

♦**Step 5** Shape the two sides, parts number 1, as shown. Make an exact pair.

♦**Step 6** Cut the ends of the nine teeth at 50 degrees as shown.

♦**Step 7** Assemble the scoop using old-style, square-cut nails, parts number 8—if you can get them. Be sure everything is square. Don't forget to add the handle *before* adding the back boards.

♦**Step 8** Glue the nine teeth in place.

♦**Step 9** Sand all over.
Since this was a tool, use a rasp to create *wear* wherever you think it would have occurred in normal use.

♦**Step 10** You can either paint or stain this project. If you want it to look old, distress it and apply a glaze top-coat. Next cranberry picking season you will be ready to pick your own!

46 ◆ Candle Sconce with Drawer

Here is a woodworking project that will add a lot to any Early American setting. It is very functional since the drawer is a great place to store matches. Every time the power went out before, I never could find matches. With this candle sconce you, too, will be ready, with a candle and matches in its drawer.

Instructions

◆**Step 1**   Study the drawing of the exploded view so that you know how it all goes together.

◆**Step 2**   Cut all of the pieces to size according to the materials list.

◆**Step 3**   Lay out the shape of the back, part number 1, and the two sides, parts number 2, using a ½-inch grid. Transfer the shapes to the wood, and cut them out. Be sure to make an exact pair of sides.

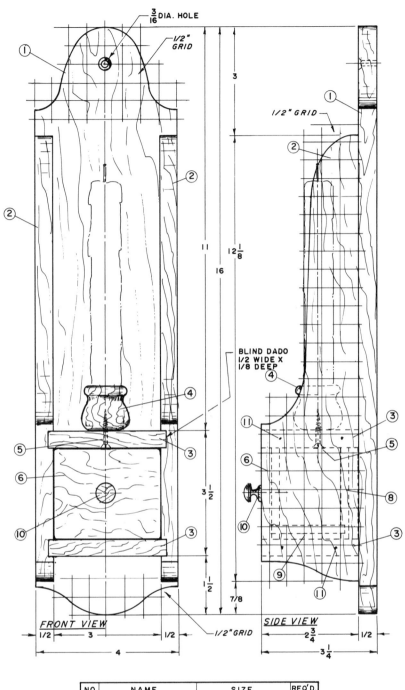

NO.	NAME	SIZE	REQ'D.
1	BACK	1/2 X 4 - 16 LONG	1
2	SIDE	1/2 X 2 3/4 - 12 1/8	2
3	SHELF	1/2 X 3 1/4 - 2 3/4	2
4	HOLDER	TO SUIT	1
5	SCREW — FL. HD.	NO. 6 - 1" LONG	1
6	FRONT	1/2 X 2 1/2 - 3 LG.	1
7	SIDE	1/4 X 2 1/2 - 2 1/2	2
8	BACK	1/4 X 2 1/2 - 2 3/4	1
9	BOTTOM	1/4 X 2 1/8 - 2 3/4	1
10	PULL	1/2 DIA.	1
11	FINISH NAIL	6d	14
12	CANDLE	TO SUIT	1

♦**Step 4** Carefully make the two "stop" dadoes, ½-inch wide and ⅛-inch deep on the *inside* surfaces of the sides. Be sure to stop the dadoes ¼ inch from the back edge. (See the exploded view on the next page.)

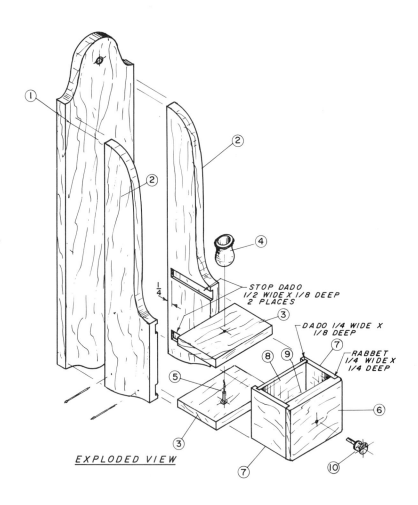

EXPLODED VIEW

◆ **Step 5**   After all of the pieces have been made, assemble the case. Check that everything is square. Be sure to screw the holder, part number 4, to the shelf, part number 3, *before* assembly.

◆ **Step 6**   Fit the drawer assembly to the case. Add the knob, part number 10.

◆ **Step 7**   This project looks great either stained or painted. Add a candle and don't forget to put matches in the drawer.

47♦Tool Box with Drawer

If *your* tool box is like mine, all the *small* tools you need are always lost in the bottom of the box. I usually have to take out two-thirds of the larger tools to find the smaller one I really need. This tool box solves that problem. Small tools go in the drawer. I wish I could take the credit for this great idea but I can't. This is a copy of an old tool box I saw in an antique shop in southern Maine.

Instructions

♦**Step 1** (The drawings are on the following pages.) Cut all of the pieces to overall size.

♦**Step 2** The center handle will have to be laid out on a 1-inch grid. Lay out the pattern, and transfer it to the wood. Cut out and round the handle area, as shown.

♦**Step 3** Locate and cut the ¾-inch-wide by ¼-inch-deep dadoes in the ends, part number 2 and 3, as shown. Note, there will be a small hole in the *bottom* surface of the dadoes after parts numbers 2,3, and 4 are assembled. This could be filled or simply left open. It will be seen after assembly.

♦**Step 4** Assemble parts number 2,3,4, and 5. Add the two sides, parts number 1, and bottom, part number 6. Since this is a tool box and will get a lot of hard use, I suggest that you glue and nail it together.

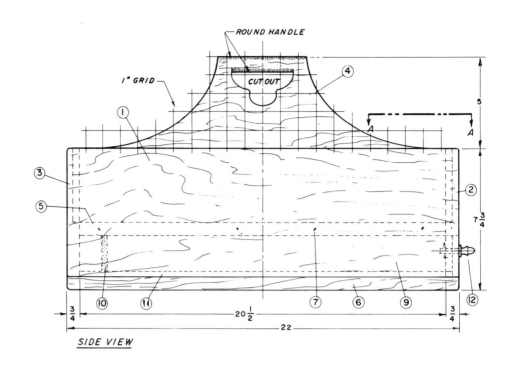

ROUND HANDLE

1" GRID

CUT OUT

SIDE VIEW

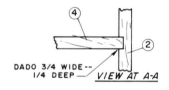

VIEW AT A-A

DADO 3/4 WIDE--
1/4 DEEP

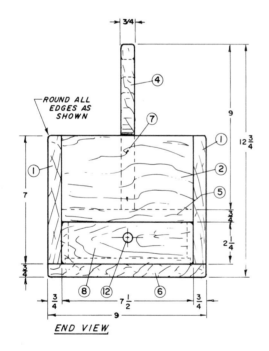

ROUND ALL
EDGES AS
SHOWN

END VIEW

NO.	NAME	SIZE	REQ'D.
1	SIDE	3/4 X 7 - 22 LONG	2
2	END	3/4 X 4 3/4 - 7 1/2 LG	1
3	END	3/4 X 7 - 7 1/2 LONG	1
4	CENTER/HANDLE	3/4 X 9 - 21 LONG	1
5	DIVIDER	3/4 X 7 1/2 - 20 1/2	1
6	BOTTOM	3/4 X 9 - 22 LONG	1
7	NAIL	6d	26
8	FRONT	3/4 X 2 1/4 - 7 1/2 LG.	1
9	SIDE	1/4 X 2 1/4 - 20 7/8 LG.	2
10	BACK	1/4 X 2 - 7 LONG	1
11	BOTTOM	1/4 X 7 - 20 7/8 LG.	1
12	PULL	5/8 DIA.	1

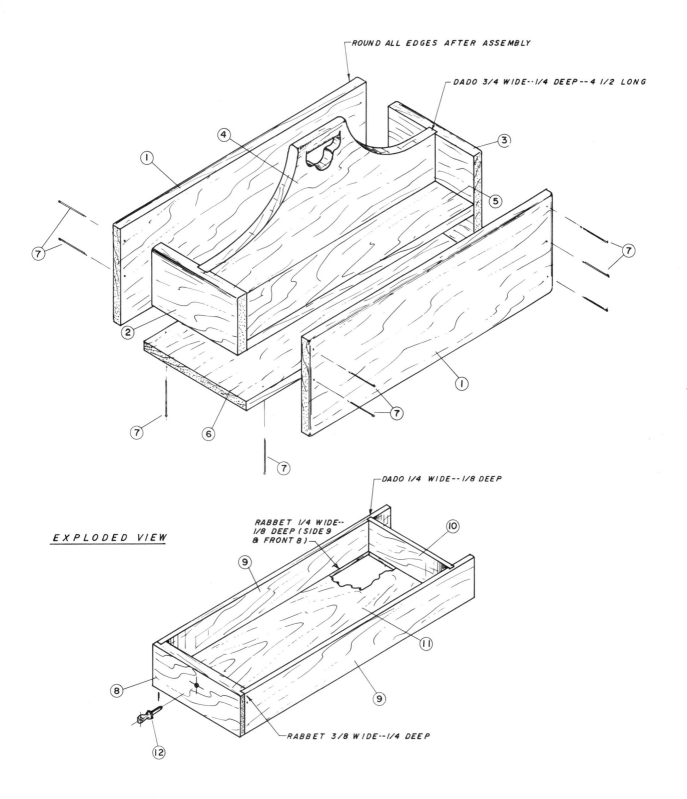

ROUND ALL EDGES AFTER ASSEMBLY

DADO 3/4 WIDE--1/4 DEEP--4 1/2 LONG

EXPLODED VIEW

DADO 1/4 WIDE--1/8 DEEP

RABBET 1/4 WIDE--1/8 DEEP (SIDE 9 & FRONT 8)

RABBET 3/8 WIDE--1/4 DEEP

◆ **Step 5** Make the drawer assembly to fit the opening, as shown. Add the pull, part number 12.

◆ **Step 6** This project can be either painted, as was the original, or stained.

48 ◆ Wall Shelf

A *cyma* curve is a curve that turns back on itself. Many Early American designs are based on a cyma curve. This colonial shelf uses a cyma curve at the top and bottom. It has graceful lines. In laying out the sides, parts number 1, locate the compass swing points; set the compass at the given radius, and draw the outer shape.

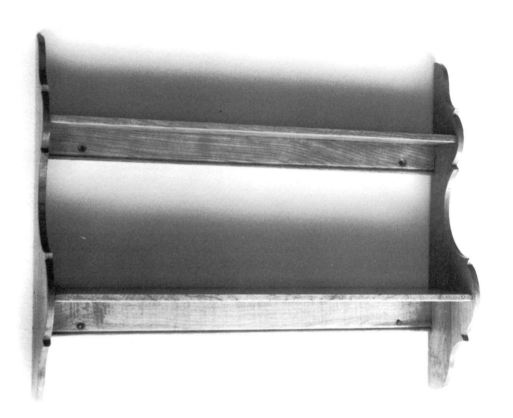

Instructions

◆**Step 1**   Lay out the shape of part 1. Transfer the pattern to the wood, and cut out the piece. It is a good idea to tape or tack the two sides together when cutting and sanding so that both sides will be exactly the same size and shape. Sand all edges.

◆**Step 2**   Cut the two shelves and brace to size. Make the ⅛-inch-radius bead in the braces, parts number 4 and 5.

◆**Step 3**   (Optional)—Cut the plate groove, if you wish, approximately ¼-inch to ⅜-inch wide and about ⅛-inch deep.

◆**Step 4**   Glue and nail the shelf together. Check that it is square.

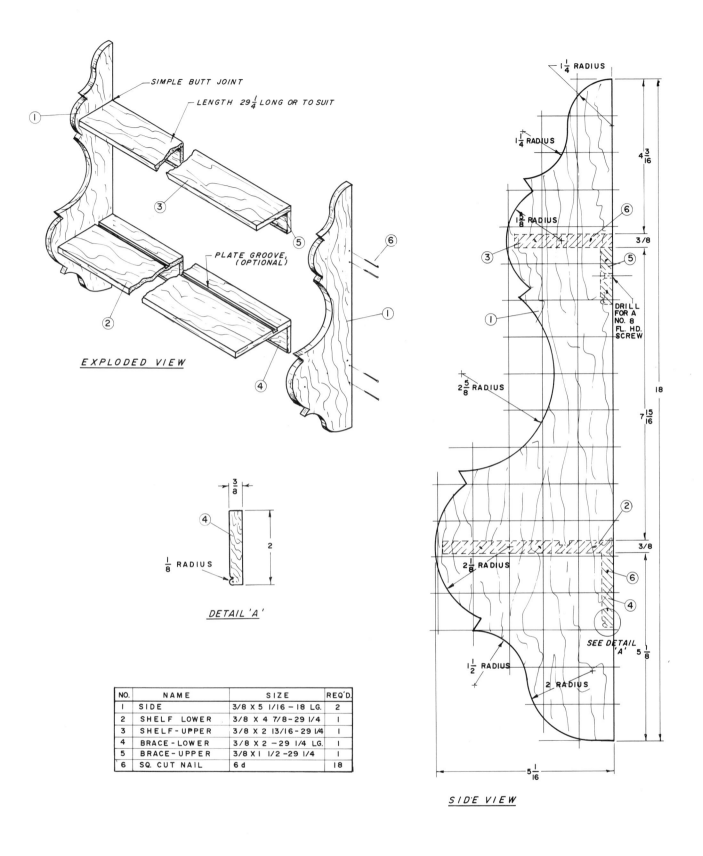

SIMPLE BUTT JOINT

LENGTH 29¼ LONG OR TO SUIT

PLATE GROOVE, (OPTIONAL)

EXPLODED VIEW

DETAIL 'A'

3/8

2

⅛ RADIUS

1¼ RADIUS

1¼ RADIUS

1⅝ RADIUS

4³⁄₁₆

3/8

DRILL FOR A NO. 8 FL. HD. SCREW

2⅝ RADIUS

18

7¹⁵⁄₁₆

2⅛ RADIUS

3/8

5⅛

SEE DETAIL 'A'

1½ RADIUS

2 RADIUS

5¹⁄₁₆

SIDE VIEW

NO.	NAME	SIZE	REQ'D.
1	SIDE	3/8 X 5 1/16 — 18 LG.	2
2	SHELF LOWER	3/8 X 4 7/8 — 29 1/4	1
3	SHELF-UPPER	3/8 X 2 13/16 — 29 1/4	1
4	BRACE-LOWER	3/8 X 2 — 29 1/4 LG.	1
5	BRACE-UPPER	3/8 X 1 1/2 — 29 1/4	1
6	SQ. CUT NAIL	6 d	18

◆**Step 5** This project is usually stained but it could be painted to blend into any room setting.

49 ♦ Tall Plant Table

Here is an old-style plant stand. I remember my Grandmother had one just like it in her "parlor." It is simple to build and will make an interesting stand for your plants. A biscuit joiner was used in making my copy, but ¼-inch-diameter dowels would work just as well.

Instructions

♦**Step 1** Cut all pieces to size. Sand all over.

♦**Step 2** Cut the *bottom* taper of the legs, parts number 1, three inches up, as shown, on the two *inside* surfaces only. Cut two slots with the biscuit joiner on the two inside surfaces as shown in the drawing of the exploded view. Sand all over.

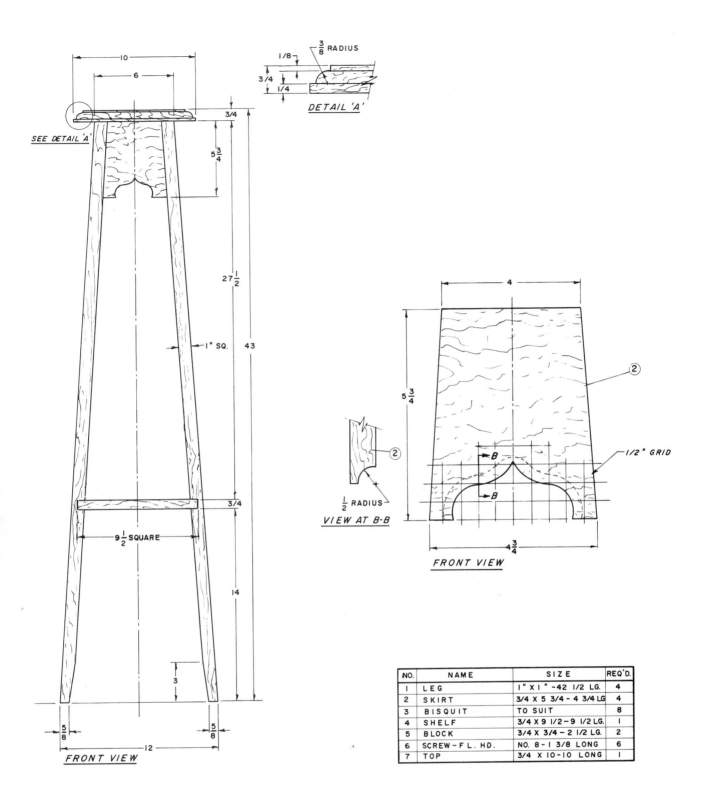

DETAIL 'A'

VIEW AT B-B

FRONT VIEW

FRONT VIEW

NO.	NAME	SIZE	REQ'D.
1	LEG	1" X 1" –42 1/2 LG.	4
2	SKIRT	3/4 X 5 3/4 – 4 3/4 LG	4
3	BISQUIT	TO SUIT	8
4	SHELF	3/4 X 9 1/2 – 9 1/2 LG.	1
5	BLOCK	3/4 X 3/4 – 2 1/2 LG.	2
6	SCREW – F L. HD.	NO. 8 – 1 3/8 LONG	6
7	TOP	3/4 X 10 – 10 LONG	1

♦ **Step 3** Lay out the skirt, part number 2. Cut two slots with the biscuit joiner to match the legs. Using a ¹⁄₂-inch-radius cove cutter with a ball-bearing follower, make a cut on the lower inside edge of the skirt to give a thin appearance. (See the drawing view at B–B.) Sand all over.

♦ **Step 4** Cut a notch following the given dimensions in all four corners of the shelf, part number 4. Sand all over. (Continued on next page.)

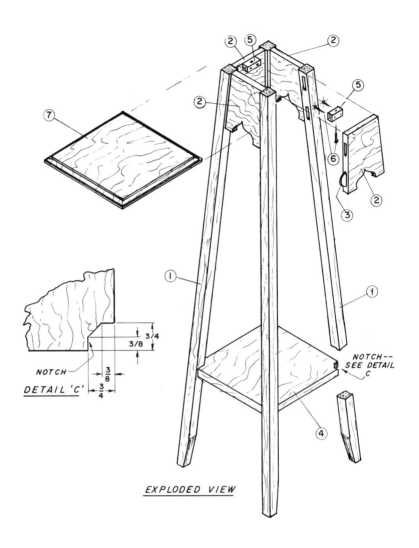

NOTCH

3/4
3/8

NOTCH

3/8
3/4

DETAIL 'C'

NOTCH --
SEE DETAIL
C

EXPLODED VIEW

♦**Step 5**   Using a router with a ³⁄₈-inch-radius round cutter, make up the top, part number 7.

♦**Step 6**   Glue the skirts, parts number 2, to the legs, parts number 1, and clamp. Check that everything is square.

♦**Step 7**   Slide the shelf, part number 4, up into place. The top surface should be about 14¾ inches above the floor. If everything is okay, glue it in place. (You might want to drill and nail it in place, if you plan to have heavy plants on the shelves.)

♦**Step 8**   Add the two blocks, parts number 5, with the screws, parts number 6.

♦**Step 9**   Screw the top, part number 7, to the blocks, part number 5. Do *not* glue in place.

♦**Step 10**   This is *another* project that could be either stained or painted. Your friends *and* plants will love this stand.

50 ♦ Child's Blanket Chest

Six-board blanket chests were one of the first things the Pilgrims brought to this country from Europe. It was, in effect, their luggage. These wonderful chests came in all shapes and sizes. Most simple ones were painted. Today, *if* and when we can find an original, it usually has two or three coats of paint on it. Note the wonderful "snipe" hinges. A very similar "snipe" can be made from four large cotter pins.

Instructions

♦ **Step 1** (The drawings are on the following pages.) Cut all pieces to overall size. If you want a real "old" look, hand-plane the front and back surfaces slightly to get a wavy effect.

♦ **Step 2** Glue and clamp wood for the 13-inch-wide front and back boards, parts number 2.

♦ **Step 3** Lay out and cut the ends, parts number 1, following the given dimensions. Don't forget to make a notch for the front and back boards.

♦ **Step 4** Glue and nail the two ends, parts number 1, to the front/back, parts number 2, and bottom, part number 3. Check that everything is square. Don't try to hide the nails; most original six-board chests were somewhat crude and the nails did show.

♦ **Step 5** Nail, but do *not* glue, the batten board, part number 5, to the lid, part number 4. (This allows for expansion of the lid.) Place them about 1/16 inch away from the sides of the chest.

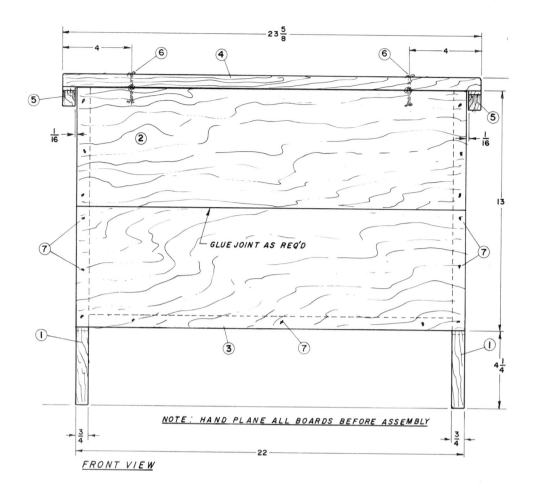

23 5/8

4 — ⑥ ④ ⑥ — 4

⑤

1/16 ② 1/16

13

⑦ GLUE JOINT AS REQ'D ⑦

⑦

① ③ ⑦ ①

4 1/4

3/4 NOTE: HAND PLANE ALL BOARDS BEFORE ASSEMBLY 3/4

22

FRONT VIEW

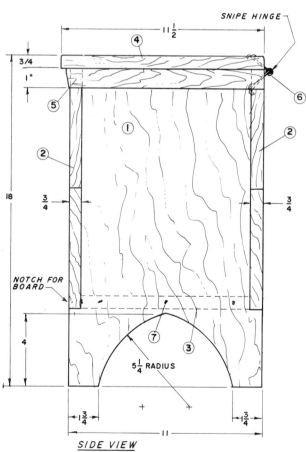

SNIPE HINGE

11 1/2

④

3/4

1" ⑤ ⑥

② ②

18

3/4 ① 3/4

② ②

NOTCH FOR
BOARD

4 ⑦

③

5 1/4 RADIUS

1 3/4 + + 1 3/4

11

SIDE VIEW

NO.	NAME	SIZE	REQ'D.
1	END BOARD	3/4 X 11 – 17 1/4 LG.	2
2	FRONT/BACK BOARD	3/4 X 13 – 22 LONG	2
3	BOTTOM BOARD	3/4 X 9 1/2 – 20 1/2	1
4	LID	3/4 X 11 1/2 – 23 5/8	1
5	BATTEN BOARD	3/4 X 1 – 11 1/4 LG.	2
6	SNIPE HINGE	COTTER PIN 1 3/4	2 PR.
7	SQ. CUT NAIL	8 d	42

146

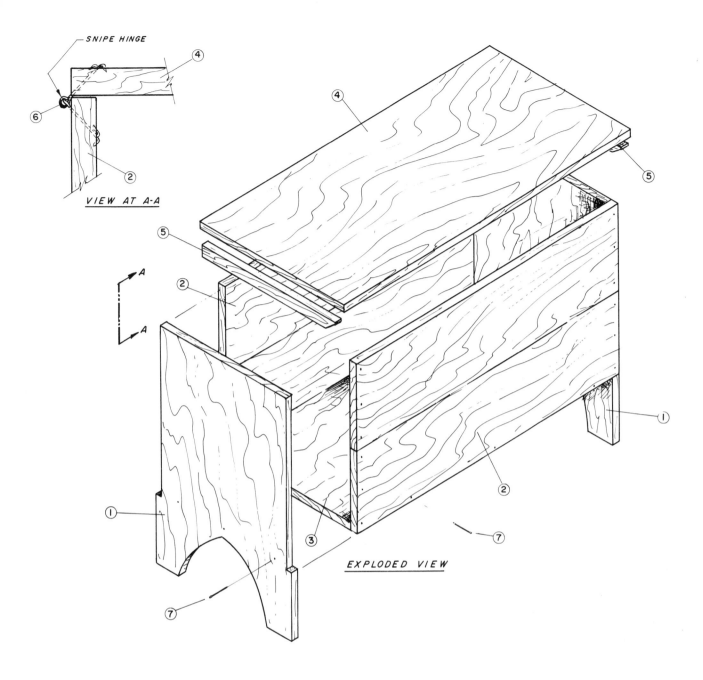

SNIPE HINGE

④

VIEW AT A-A

EXPLODED VIEW

◆**Step 6**   Using a drill, drill holes at about 45 degrees as shown in the drawing at view A–A. Assemble two cotter pins, and place them into the holes; one into the lid and the other into the back board. Temporarily drive them in a little deeper than you think you need, and then with a pair of needle-nose pliers, loop the tips of the cotter pins around and down into the wood. Hammer them down into the wood. This will make a slightly loose fit, but it will look very original. (If you don't like snipe hinges, a regular pair of brass butt hinges can be used.)

◆**Step 7**   Sand all over. Since you want this to be "old," round edges where you feel wear would have occurred.

◆**Step 8**   Paint or stain to suit. As I like an old-looking blanket chest, I distressed mine and painted it two different colors, on top of each other. Sand down through the top coat here and there to show the first color. If you really want it to look old use a crackle coat, and a top-coat of a black wash.

51 ◆ Chippendale Mirror

The Chippendale period, as we now designate it, was from 1750 to 1785. The name derives from Thomas Chippendale of London, England, whose book of 1754 titled *The Gentleman and Cabinet Maker's Directory* widely popularized the furniture style characterized by graceful outline and ornate or elaborate ornamentation. It was the most complete and comprehensive furniture manual that had ever been published. The book provided inspiration for craftsmen in the American colony as well as in many other countries throughout the world.

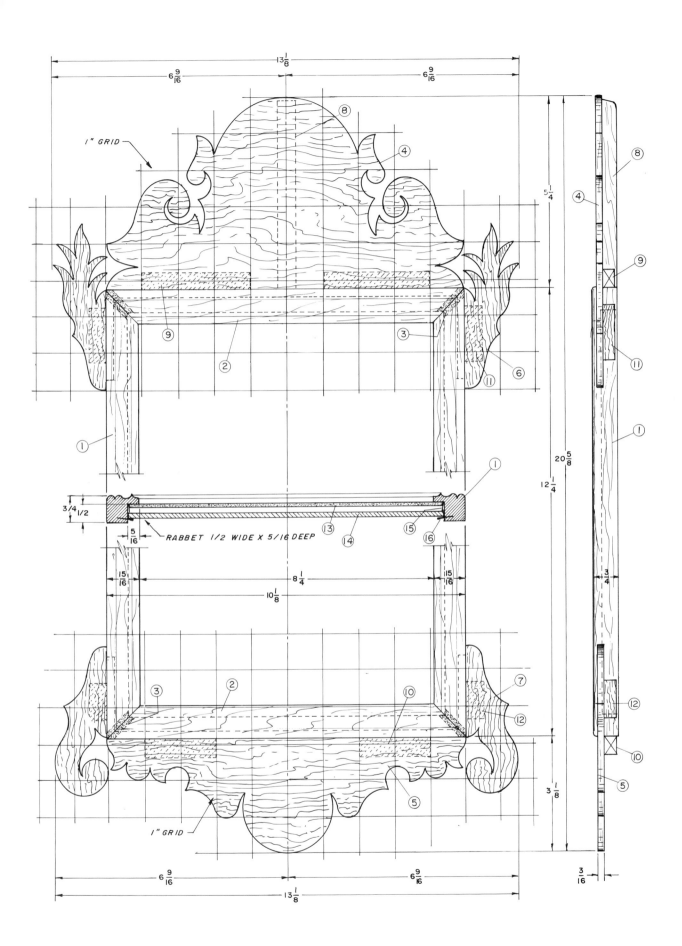

(Continued on following pages.)

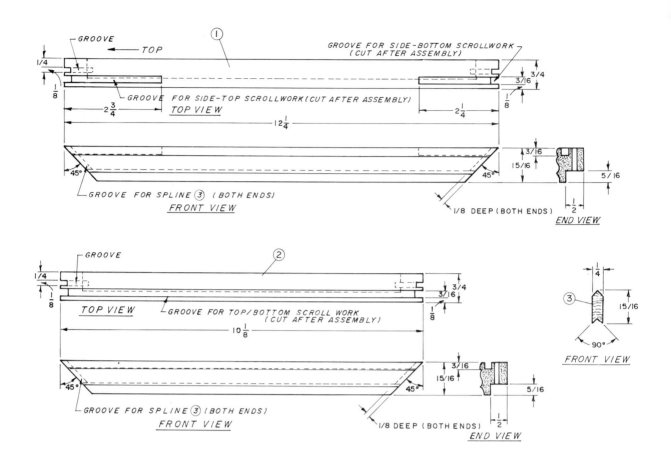

The moulding profile of the top, bottom, and sides of the frame can be made using a combination of router or shaper bits. If you plan to make many mirrors for resale, you might want to have a custom router bit made up. These are not very expensive and will save a lot of time and do a very professional job.

Instructions

◆**Step 1** Cut all of the pieces to overall size according to the materials list. Sand all surfaces down with a fine grit of sandpaper; this will save you from having to do a lot of finish-sanding later.

◆**Step 2** Cut the moulding profile shape of the face of the top, bottom, and two sides. (It is a good idea to make a few extra pieces just in case you make an error cutting.) Make the rabbet cut in the back according to the plans for the mirror.

◆**Step 3** Make exact 45-degree mitre cuts at the ends of the top, bottom, and side pieces as shown in the plans.

◆**Step 4** Glue the frame together. Be sure to keep all of the corners at *exactly* 90 degrees. After the glue sets, cut notches for the top, bottom, and side scrolls, as shown in the drawings. Refer carefully to the plans as you make the project.

◆**Step 5** On a sheet of paper draw a ½-inch grid. Lay out the top, bottom, and side scrolls. Transfer each pattern to the wood.

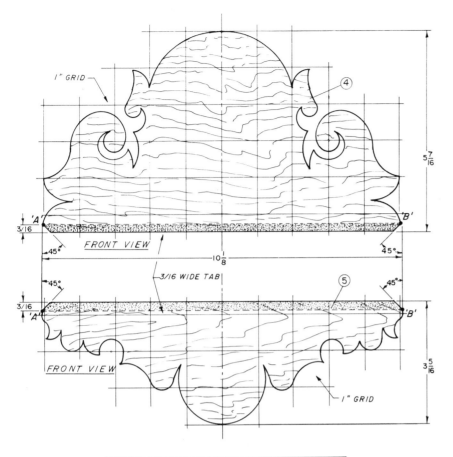

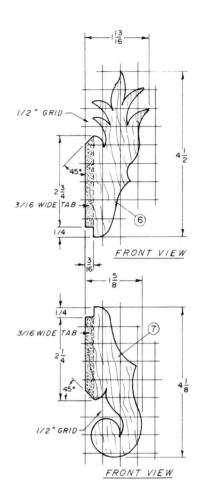

NO.	NAME	SIZE	REQ'D.
1	SIDE	3/4 X 15/16 -12 1/4 LG.	2
2	TOP-BOTTOM	3/4 X 15/16 -10 1/8 LG.	2
3	SPLINE	1/8 X 1/4 -15/16 LG	4
4	TOP SCROLL	3/16 X 5 7/16 -10 1/8	1
5	BOTTOM SCROLL	3/16 X 3 5/16 -10 1/8	1
6	TOP/SIDE SCROLL	3/16 X 1 13/16- 4 1/2	2
7	BOTTOM/SIDE SCROLL	3/16 X 1 5/8 - 4 1/8	2
8	BRACE	7/16 X 1/2 -5 1/8 LG.	1
9	BLOCK TOP	3/8 X 1/2 - 3 LONG	2
10	BLOCK BOTTOM	3/8 X 1/2 - 2 LONG	2
11	BLOCK TOP/SIDE	3/8 X 1/2 - 1 1/2 LG.	2
12	BLOCK BOTTOM/SIDE	3/8 X 1/2 - 1 LONG	2
13	MIRROR	3/32 X 8 13/16 -10 15/16	1
14	BACK BOARD	1/4 X 8 7/8 -11 LONG	1
15	WEDGE	1/8 X 1/8 -3/8 LG	8
16	FINISH NAIL	3/4 LONG	8

Important: Before cutting out, check that the distance across the mirror frame is *exactly* the same dimension as your scroll patterns. *This is very important.* Carefully cut out the top and bottom scroll.

◆**Step 6** All that is left to do now is to glue the scroll(s) to the frame subassembly. After the glue sets, add the brace(s).

◆**Step 7** Resand all over using very fine sandpaper. Then, cut the back board to size according to the plans. Sand all over once again.

◆**Step 8** Apply a stain of your choice as you wish. If you use a wood such as walnut, mahogany, or even cherry, you may not want to apply a stain. Apply four or five satin finish top-coats such as tung oil. Lightly sand between coats using 0000 steel wool. Add a coat of paste wax and your mirror frame is ready for the mirror. (Continued on next page.)

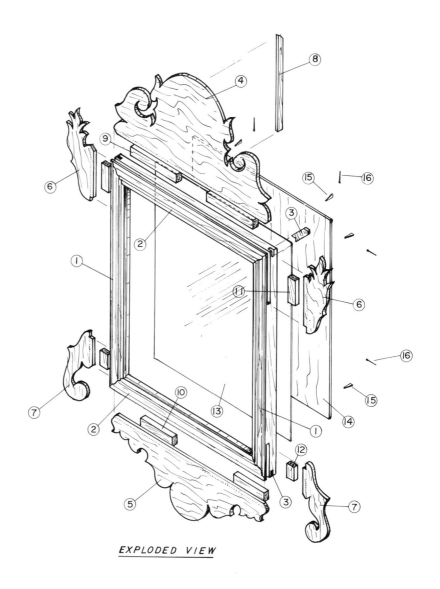

EXPLODED VIEW

◆ **Step 9** Add the mirror and back board, as shown, with square-cut finish nails.

◆ **Step 10** Clean and polish the mirror, and your wall mirror is ready to sell or hang, perfect for any room.

52♦Round Plant Stand

Whenever I am visiting antique shops, I invariably find an old plant stand now and then. Most have little tags on them noting *"not for sale."* Plant stands such as this one are very scarce, so the dealers do *not* want to sell them. They use them for display only. I have made all kinds—four-legged table types (like Project No. 50), half-round—but *this* is my first round plant stand. It is very unusual. The extra braces, parts number 5, really make it different.

Instructions

♦**Step 1**   On a board ¾ inch by 6½ inches and 41½ inches long, carefully lay out the leg, part number 1, following the given dimensions.

Note: All surfaces labeled with an "X" are *parallel* to each other. Those labeled with a "Y" are also *parallel* to each other and 90 degrees from those at "X." (Notice that it is drawn upside down.)

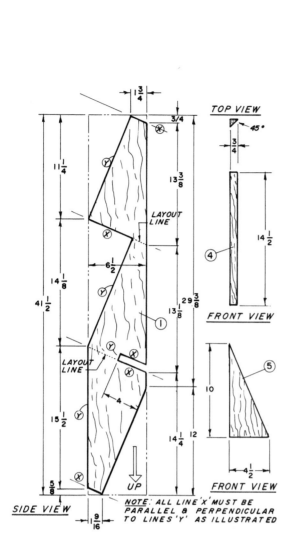

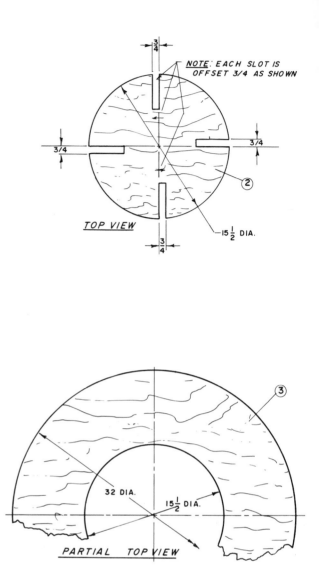

♦ **Step 2** Cut out the four legs. If you have a band saw, tack the four legs together and cut them all out at once.

♦ **Step 3** Lay out and cut to size the center and bottom shelf, parts number 2 and 3. Sand all over. You probably will have to glue up a board 32 inches square in order to cut out the bottom shelf, part number 3.

♦ **Step 4** Cut to size the spacers, parts number 5, brace, part number 6, and top shelf, part number 7.

♦ **Step 5** Dry-fit all pieces. If everything is okay, glue and nail the four legs, parts number 1, to the bottom shelf, part number 3. Glue and nail the center shelf, part number 2, in place.

♦ **Step 6** Add the spacers, parts number 4. Add the top brace, part number 5.

♦ **Step 7** Add the top shelf, part number 6, and you're done, except for finishing. (Continued on following pages.)

154

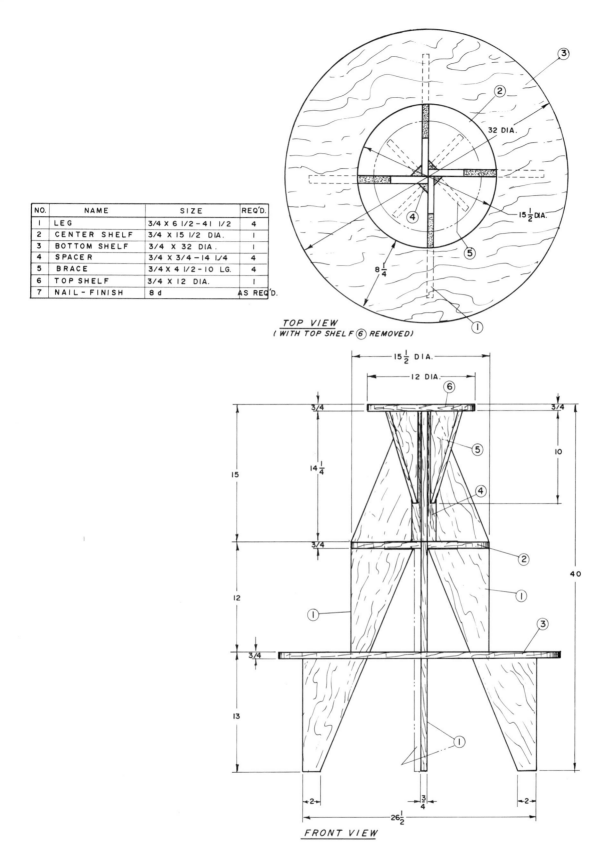

NO.	NAME	SIZE	REQ'D.
I	LEG	3/4 X 6 1/2 – 41 1/2	4
2	CENTER SHELF	3/4 X 15 1/2 DIA.	I
3	BOTTOM SHELF	3/4 X 32 DIA.	I
4	SPACER	3/4 X 3/4 – 14 1/4	4
5	BRACE	3/4 X 4 1/2 – 10 LG.	4
6	TOP SHELF	3/4 X 12 DIA.	I
7	NAIL – FINISH	8 d	AS REQ'D.

TOP VIEW
(WITH TOP SHELF ⑥ REMOVED)

FRONT VIEW

(Exploded view is on next page.)

155

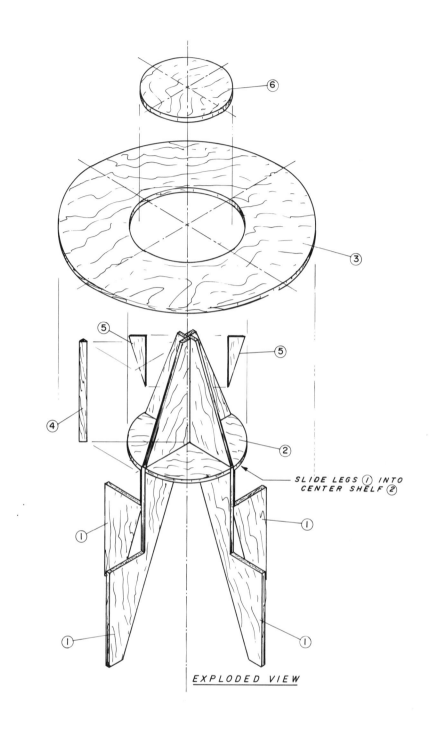

EXPLODED VIEW

SLIDE LEGS ① INTO
CENTER SHELF ②

♦ **Step 8** This project can be either stained or painted. Most old ones were
painted. I found in my travels those from Vermont were stained *and* painted.
The legs, spacers, and braces were painted; the three shelves were stained
and varnished. Personally, I like the "Vermont" touch, and I like to distress
the shelves to make the stand look old. All you need now is a bright corner
that needs a plant stand and a lot of plants.

Solution for Nail Puzzle

Project 3, pages 22 and 23

Solution: See the four steps below.

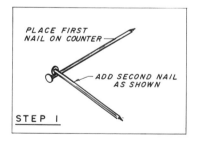

PLACE FIRST
NAIL ON COUNTER

ADD SECOND NAIL
AS SHOWN

STEP 1

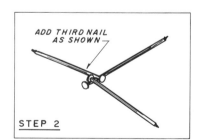

ADD THIRD NAIL
AS SHOWN

STEP 2

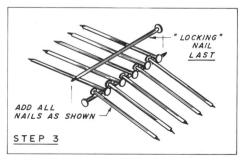

"LOCKING"
NAIL
LAST

ADD ALL
NAILS AS SHOWN

STEP 3

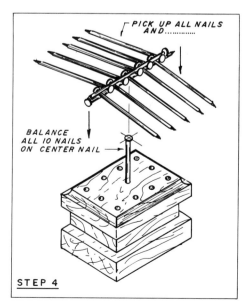

PICK UP ALL NAILS
AND............

BALANCE
ALL 10 NAILS
ON CENTER NAIL

STEP 4

Metric Conversion

Inches to Millimetres and Centimetres

MM—millimetres   CM—centimetres

Inches	MM	CM	Inches	CM	Inches	CM
⅛	3	0.3	9	22.9	30	76.2
¼	6	0.6	10	25.4	31	78.7
⅜	10	1.0	11	27.9	32	81.3
½	13	1.3	12	30.5	33	83.8
⅝	16	1.6	13	33.0	34	86.4
¾	19	1.9	14	35.6	35	88.9
⅞	22	2.2	15	38.1	36	91.4
1	25	2.5	16	40.6	37	94.0
1¼	32	3.2	17	43.2	38	96.5
1½	38	3.8	18	45.7	39	99.1
1¾	44	4.4	19	48.3	40	101.6
2	51	5.1	20	50.8	41	104.1
2½	64	6.4	21	53.3	42	106.7
3	76	7.6	22	55.9	43	109.2
3½	89	8.9	23	58.4	44	111.8
4	102	10.2	24	61.0	45	114.3
4½	114	11.4	25	63.5	46	116.8
5	127	12.7	26	66.0	47	119.4
6	152	15.2	27	68.6	48	121.9
7	178	17.8	28	71.1	49	124.5
8	203	20.3	29	73.7	50	127.0

Index